HENRIK IBSEN

Born in Norway in 1828, Ibsen began his writing career with romantic history plays influenced by Shakespeare and Schiller. In 1851 he was appointed writer-in-residence at the newly established Norwegian Theatre in Bergen with a contract to write a play a year for five years, following which he was made Artistic Director of the Norwegian Theatre in what is now Oslo. In the 1860s he moved abroad to concentrate wholly on writing. He began with two mighty verse dramas, *Brand* and *Peer Gynt*, and in the 1870s and 1880s wrote the sequence of realistic 'problem' plays for which he is best known, among them *A Doll's House*, *Ghosts*, *An Enemy of the People*, *Hedda Gabler* and *Rosmersholm*. His last four plays, *The Master Builder*, *Little Eyolf*, *John Gabriel Borkman* and *When We Dead Awaken*, dating from his return to Norway in the 1890s, are increasingly overlaid with symbolism. Illness forced him to retire in 1900, and he died in 1906 after a series of crippling strokes.

ELINOR COOK

Elinor Cook was the winner of the George Devine Award for Most Promising Playwright in 2013.

Her plays include *Out of Love* (Paines Plough/Theatr Clwyd/Orange Tree); *Extra Yarn* (Orange Tree); *Pilgrims* (HighTide/Theatr Clwyd/The Yard); *The Rehearsal* (LAMDA); *Ten Weeks* (Paines Plough/Royal Welsh College of Music and Drama); *Image of an Unknown Young Woman* (Gate); *The Boy Preference* (NT Connections); *The Girl's Guide to Saving The World* (HighTide); *this is where we got to when you came in* (Bush/non zero one). She wrote an episode of *The Secrets* for BBC One, directed by Dominic Savage.

Henrik Ibsen

THE LADY FROM THE SEA

in a new version by
Elinor Cook

NICK HERN BOOKS

London
www.nickhernbooks.co.uk

A Nick Hern Book

This version of *The Lady from the Sea* first published in Great Britain in 2017 as a paperback original by Nick Hern Books Limited, The Glasshouse, 49a Goldhawk Road, London W12 8QP

This version of *The Lady from the Sea* copyright © 2017 Elinor Cook

Elinor Cook has asserted her right to be identified as the author of this version

Cover photograph of Nikki Amuka-Bird by Daniel Kennedy

Designed and typeset by Nick Hern Books, London
Printed in Great Britain by Mimeo Ltd, Huntingdon, Cambridgeshire PE29 6XX

A CIP catalogue record for this book is available from the British Library

ISBN 978 1 84842 718 1

This version of *The Lady from the Sea* was first performed at the Donmar Warehouse, London, on 18 October 2017 (previews from 12 October), with the following cast, in order of speaking:

BALLESTRED	Jim Findley
BOLETTE	Helena Wilson
LYNGSTRAND	Jonny Holden
HILDE	Ellie Bamber
DOCTOR WANGEL	Finbar Lynch
ARNHOLM	Tom Mckay
ELLIDA	Nikki Amuka-Bird
THE STRANGER	Jake Fairbrother

Director	Kwame Kwei-Armah
Designer	Tom Scutt
Lighting Designer	Lee Curran
Sound Designer	Emma Laxton
Composer	Michael Bruce

Acknowledgements

My heartfelt thanks to Josie Rourke, Kate Pakenham,
Al Coomer, Lynette Linton, Fay Davies, Tumi Belo,
Sarah Liisa Wilkinson, Tom Doyle, Alice Stevenson and to
Lesley, Jeremy and Richard Cook.

Extra special thanks to Nikki Amuka-Bird, Clare Slater and
Kwame Kwei-Armah for being so generous with their time and
insightful with their thoughts.

E.C.

'Love is a deadly business. It throws us up against ourselves, leaves us hanging there.'

Vivian Gornick

Characters

ELLIDA
DOCTOR WANGEL
BOLETTE
HILDE
ARNHOLM
LYNGSTRAND
BALLESTRED
THE STRANGER

This text went to press before the end of rehearsals and so may differ slightly from the play as performed.

ACT ONE

The arbour of DOCTOR WANGEL'*s garden, at the back of an old colonial wooden house, on a leafy hill, on a Caribbean island, sometime in the mid-1950s.*

The garden is fragrant with jasmine, hibiscus and bougainvillea.

A path can be seen, which leads to a deep, almost frighteningly dark lagoon.

There are large tamarind trees at the edges of the garden, and a fence.

Just outside the fence, there is an artist's easel and a box of watercolours.

BALLESTRED *is attempting to hoist a large flag.*

BOLETTE, *who is carrying an embarrassment of flowers, is watching him.*

BALLESTRED   Like that?

BOLETTE   Sort of…

BALLESTRED   It's a bit tricky…

BOLETTE   You're nearly there.
Keep going…
That's it!
It looks much better now, doesn't it?
Like we're really celebrating something.

They look at the flag, pleased.

BALLESTRED   Are you expecting a guest?
The governor himself, I'd imagine, with all this finery…

BOLETTE	Um.
	Beat.
	You might remember Mr Arnholm.
BALLESTRED	Rings a bell… Clever chap. With the big books and the geometry set.
BOLETTE	That's him. He's been in Europe the last eight years… This will be the first time he's set foot on the island since 1943.
BALLESTRED	Wasn't he your tutor?
BOLETTE	Well, yes. But. He's more of a friend than anything else.
BALLESTRED	To your father?
BOLETTE	To all of us.
	LYNGSTRAND *enters.*
LYNGSTRAND	Hello…?
BOLETTE	(*To* BALLESTRED.) Hold these, will you?
	She thrusts a bunch of flowers into BALLESTRED*'s hands and turns hastily* *away from* LYNGSTRAND.
LYNGSTRAND	Your mother said I should come and visit, if I was passing. And I was. So…
BOLETTE	Right. Yes.
	She stares at LYNGSTRAND *for a moment,* *unsure what to say.*
	More flowers. There aren't enough flowers.

LYNGSTRAND *looks at the riot of flowers around him.*

LYNGSTRAND Um...?

BOLETTE *hurries inside.*

BALLESTRED Could I just cheat you that way a moment?

LYNGSTRAND What?

BALLESTRED You're in my light.

LYNGSTRAND *moves reluctantly out of the way.*

He wanders over to the easel, peers at BALLESTRED*'s painting.*

LYNGSTRAND Charming...

BALLESTRED It's the waterfall.
At the lagoon.

LYNGSTRAND Yes, I'd worked that out.

BALLESTRED Although obviously I'm not going to leave it just like that!

LYNGSTRAND Oh good...

BALLESTRED I'm going to add a figure.
Here.

LYNGSTRAND Yes I think it needs it.

BALLESTRED A mermaid.
They say she lives at the bottom of the lagoon.
Lures men to their deaths.

LYNGSTRAND Oh that old myth...

BALLESTRED She'll be sprawled on the rocks, here, gasping for breath.
The waterfall will be crashing all around her.
Beating relentlessly down on her head!

LYNGSTRAND Could work...

BALLESTRED   She's trying to stem the flow of it with her
              hands but it's no use!
              The poor mermaid is doomed.

LYNGSTRAND   How did she end up on the rocks?

BALLESTRED   A storm tossed her there.
              And now she's too weak to heave herself back
              into the water.
              So she's trapped.
              Struggling to catch her breath, as it ebbs
              away…

LYNGSTRAND   What are you going to call it?

BALLESTRED   'The Mermaid's Last Gasp.'

LYNGSTRAND   Oh, no.
              You need something colder.
              Cleaner.
              Like – 'Mermaid, Exhales.'

BALLESTRED   Are you in the business too?
              You seem to have a lot of opinions…

LYNGSTRAND   Oh I'm not interested in watercolours.
              But I'm certainly an artist.
              A sculptor, actually.

BALLESTRED   A fine artistic practice.
              Very different to painting of course, rather
              blunter perhaps, but…

LYNGSTRAND   I'm trying to disrupt the practice, actually.
              Carve out a new artistic form.
              I'm Hans Lyngstrand, by the way.
              You might have heard of me.

BALLESTRED   I don't think so.

LYNGSTRAND   There have been quite a few pieces about me
              in various journals.
              Some rather well-respected publications,
              in fact.

BALLESTRED   Must have missed them.
              I've definitely seen you about though.

LYNGSTRAND   I doubt it.
              Mostly I stay in my studio.
              Working.

BALLESTRED   Oh yes, now I remember.
              You're the sickly one.

LYNGSTRAND   What?

BALLESTRED   You're in luck.
              The island is good for healing.

LYNGSTRAND   I'm just recovering from a chest infection.
              A nasty one.
              But it's nothing serious.

BALLESTRED   You do look a bit peaky.
              Perhaps you need to poke your head out of
              that studio a little more frequently.

LYNGSTRAND   Oh no, I'm good as new now, practically.
              But I'm hoping for a consultation with
              Dr Wangel.
              Just to be sure.

BALLESTRED   A very fine doctor.
              Oh look.
              Yet another speedboat zipping into view.
              Do you see?
              Any moment now the tourists will be
              disgorged and…
              Ah!
              There.
              Didn't I tell you?

LYNGSTRAND   Is the lady of the house in…?

BALLESTRED   Look at all that garish blue and pink and
              turquoise…
              The mandatory colours for holidaying in the
              Caribbean.
              You've resisted that, I see.

LYNGSTRAND   I don't really consider myself a tourist...

BALLESTRED   Look, there they go.
Streaming off the boats and stuffing
themselves into the bars and cafés of the
Marina.
And there are the taxis, look.
Lined up like ants, waiting to take them to
The Viceroy, The Royal Palms, The Meridian.

LYNGSTRAND   I can't stand those ghastly places.
I'm after a much more authentic experience.

BALLESTRED   They're not interested in authenticity.
Or, they are.
But only in its most palatable form.
Preferably with a rum cocktail in hand and the
locals only visible as smiling waiting staff.
In pristine uniforms.

LYNGSTRAND   Spoken like a true local.

BALLESTRED   Oh I've only been here twenty years myself!
I arrived with the Golden Beach Amateur
Dramatics Society.
We brought our radical reworking of *The
Taming of the Shrew*.
Perhaps you've heard of it...?
Well, no.
The GBADS doesn't exist any more.
More's the pity.
We hit a bit of financial difficulty.
Such is life!
And it's certainly not the worst place to find
yourself in penury.
Paradise!

LYNGSTRAND   Sounds like you landed on your feet.

BALLESTRED   Oh I've earned my keep.
I was in the decorating business back then,
of course.

I'd give all the verandas in the neighbourhood
a nice lick of paint when the sun had bleached
them to a crisp.
Lovely work!
Sociable too...

BOLETTE *enters*.

BOLETTE   Hilde!
Have you got the chair for Dad?

HILDE   (*Off*.) Get it yourself!

LYNGSTRAND   (*To* BOLETTE.) There you are!
I didn't get a chance to say hello properly
before, you were in such a rush!

BOLETTE   Um, yes, sorry, it's just...
Hilde!
Hilde – !

BOLETTE *exits*.

BALLESTRED   You seem to have made some friends...

LYNGSTRAND   Mrs Wangel said I was welcome any time
I wanted.

BALLESTRED   Well, you're in luck.
They're very good people to know.
Very well regarded.
Now, much as I'd love to stay and chat I have
some very droopy curls to attend to.

LYNGSTRAND   I'm sorry?

BALLESTRED   A lady's relationship with her hair is
extremely fraught.
The amount they moan about the humidity!
The dismay on their faces when their poodle
cuts and pageboys sag around their chins!
Still, it keeps me out of mischief!

LYNGSTRAND   Ah.
So hairdressing is your real profession.

BALLESTRED   I turn my hand to all sorts of things.
               I'm a true Renaissance man.
               You could use a trim yourself, actually.
               I'll do you a very competitive price.
               Just ask for Ballestred, the dance teacher!

LYNGSTRAND   Dance teacher?

BALLESTRED   Oh yes.
               I teach the Merengue and the Rhumba.
               The ladies adore me.
               Their husbands aren't so keen.
               Ha!
               Oh and I should also mention that I'm in
               a little percussion group as well.
               I play the pan drums.
               Badly, but we persevere…!
               We've got a concert this evening in fact, up at
               The Heights.
               Very informal.
               Very lively bunch.
               You should come.
               Very much your thing, I should think.
               Goodbye!

               BALLESTRED *exits*.

               HILDE *enters*.

               Looks at LYNGSTRAND.

HILDE   You're sweating.

LYNGSTRAND   Oh, it's you.

HILDE   You should invest in some lighter clothes.
               If you insist on striding around in the
               midday sun.

               BOLETTE *enters with more flowers*.

LYNGSTRAND   I haven't been striding anywhere.
               I went for a swim down at the lagoon, that's all.
               Your mother was there.

HILDE	Who?
LYNGSTRAND	(*To* BOLETTE.) Won't you sit down? All this rushing can't be good for anyone!
BOLETTE	You didn't see Father on your way here, did you?
LYNGSTRAND	I think I saw his boat out on the lakes...
BOLETTE	He'll be here soon, in that case. Hilde, did you bring his chair, like I asked?
HILDE	No.
LYNGSTRAND	Are you having a party or something? It's not your father's birthday, is it? I wish you'd said. I'd have brought him something.
HILDE	Not Dad's birthday, no.
BOLETTE	Hilde.
HILDE	Mum's though. Good old Mummy!
BOLETTE	Hilde, shut up.
HILDE	(*To* LYNGSTRAND.) You're not expecting to stay for lunch, I hope.
LYNGSTRAND	Oh. No. I'll wander back to my digs and see what Mrs Jensen can rustle up.
HILDE	Mrs Jensen? You poor creature.
LYNGSTRAND	Not at all. She understands my needs.
HILDE	Which are?
LYNGSTRAND	Solitude, mostly. Absolute quiet.

HILDE   What for?

LYNGSTRAND My work, of course.

BOLETTE   Mr Lyngstrand is quite the artistic sensation.

LYNGSTRAND Well, there's no need to exaggerate...

BOLETTE   Hans is a sculptor on the cusp of stardom.
               About to hit the big time in New York.

HILDE   Oh New York.
               Ugh.

LYNGSTRAND (*To* BOLETTE.) Have you ever been?

HILDE   She's never even left the region!

BOLETTE   (*To* HILDE.) Neither have you.

HILDE   At least I don't keep talking and talking
               about it.

BOLETTE   I will leave.
               Soon.

HILDE   When?

BOLETTE   Whenever I want.

HILDE   When?
               This afternoon?
               Tomorrow?
               When, Bolette?

               WANGEL *enters*.

WANGEL   Where are my favourite daughters?

BOLETTE   Dad!
               You're back.

WANGEL   Of course.
               I told you I'd be here for lunch.

               He embraces BOLETTE *and glances at his*
               watch.

               She notices the gesture.

BOLETTE	How long do we have you for today?
WANGEL	Well… I should really head back in an hour or so. There was quite a stream of ailments this morning. Even a thrilling dislocated shoulder.
BOLETTE	Oh, but…!
WANGEL	Don't you want your old father to be occupied?
BOLETTE	No, yes, of course… It's just –
HILDE	Do you think the garden looks nice, Dad?
WANGEL	It's certainly… eye-catching.
BOLETTE	But you like it though? Don't you?
WANGEL	Let's hope Arnholm doesn't have hayfever.
HILDE	It's not for Arnholm.
WANGEL	What?
BOLETTE	(*To* HILDE.) Shut. Up.
HILDE	What did I say?!
WANGEL	He hasn't arrived yet, has he?
BOLETTE	He came in on the ship last night.
WANGEL	Wonderful. We can expect him any minute in that case. Has there been any… Any sign of Ellida?
BOLETTE	She's down at the lagoon.
WANGEL	Ah yes of course. Of course.

He glances at the flag.

We've got the flag flying as well, have we?

BOLETTE	It looks festive, don't you think…?
WANGEL	My loves, aren't all these decorations a bit excessive?
HILDE	You didn't mind last year.
WANGEL	Last year?
BOLETTE	No, that's not why we're –
HILDE	Yes it is.
WANGEL	Girls!

They look at him.

You've done a glorious job.
It's a beautiful tribute to…
To someone we miss…
Very much.

BOLETTE	Dad, it's all right.
WANGEL	I want to remember her too.
But I wish you'd be honest with me about it.
BOLETTE	We're sorry…
WANGEL	You shouldn't be organising something like this behind my back.
It's not right.
And, more importantly, it's not fair on…

Silence.

I'm sorry.
Forget I said anything.
It's lovely that you do this every year.
I shouldn't have interfered.
Rituals matter.

BOLETTE	We're sorry, Dad.
We'll take it down…
HILDE	Oh – !
BOLETTE	Hilde, see if you can get the flag down –

WANGEL	No. Please. Leave it just as it is.
BOLETTE	You're sure?
WANGEL	I'm sure. Although – Ellida hasn't seen it, has she?
BOLETTE	No.
WANGEL	No. Good. I'll try and speak to her before –
HILDE	God, is that Mr Arnholm?
BOLETTE	Where?
HILDE	Look.
BOLETTE	Of course that's not him.
WANGEL	Arnholm! Over here!
BOLETTE	But...
HILDE	He's limping!
BOLETTE	He isn't. Not really...
HILDE	I wish I could have fought in the war. I'd have killed so many Germans.
WANGEL	Need a hand, Arnholm?
	ARNHOLM *enters, with a cane.*
ARNHOLM	No, no! Don't worry! Looks much worse than it is!
WANGEL	Give him a hand, Bolette.
ARNHOLM	Good Lord. I hope this finery isn't all for me!

HILDE	Don't worry. It isn't.
ARNHOLM	That can't be Hilde, can it?
HILDE	Why not?
ARNHOLM	You were nine years old the last time I saw you. Exploding everything you could get your hands on with your chemistry set.
HILDE	Ugh!
WANGEL	Hilde finds nothing more mortifying than being reminded she was once a child.
HILDE	Dad!

BOLETTE tentatively goes to ARNHOLM.

BOLETTE	Um, do you want a hand?
ARNHOLM	Thank you, Bolette.

They look at each other for a second.

This is…
This is quite a transformation.

They hold their gaze for a moment.

Then BOLETTE *looks away, unbearably uncomfortable.*

Well!
Nothing like seeing your former students to
make you feel ancient.
I'd forgotten how steep that path is!

He fans himself with his hat.

BOLETTE	I'll get you something to drink.
ARNHOLM	No, no –
WANGEL	I think some brandy would be just the thing.
BOLETTE	Perhaps… Perhaps just some soda…

WANGEL	Brandy and soda. An excellent idea. Would you mind, Bolette?

After a moment of hesitation, she turns in the direction of the house.

BOLETTE	Of course.
ARNHOLM	(*To* BOLETTE.) I hope you'll come and sit with us when you have a chance?
BOLETTE	Maybe later.

BOLETTE exits.

HILDE looks at WANGEL and ARNHOLM.

HILDE	I'll sit with you.
WANGEL	Hilde. Would you mind putting my bag in the study?
HILDE	Yes I would.
WANGEL	Hilde...

After a moment, HILDE exits, huffily.

ARNHOLM	Good Lord. You've got two grown women in your house.
WANGEL	They're still just children.
ARNHOLM	I wouldn't be so sure...
WANGEL	Don't rush me, Arnholm. Indulge a fond old man.

Pause.

We all missed you when you went, you know.
Of course, it was rather a different house.
Then.

ARNHOLM	Yes...

Pause.

I was so very sorry to hear about…
About your first wife.

WANGEL   Yes.
           It was all…
           All rather a shock when Claudia got so ill
           and…

ARNHOLM   I can imagine.

WANGEL   It still feels so fresh, even all these years later.

ARNHOLM   Yes.

WANGEL   But, of course, I'm so happy now.
           So happy.

ARNHOLM   I'm –
           Delighted to hear it.

WANGEL   How could anyone fail to be happy here?

ARNHOLM   Yes.
           Yes.

WANGEL   The house is looking so lovely.
           The garden is flourishing.
           Business is…
           Ticking along.
           The girls are well.

ARNHOLM   And of course, you've got Ellida.
           Your new wife…

           Pause.

WANGEL   Yes.
           I'm very fortunate.

ARNHOLM   You know, we…
           We knew one another before.
           I started my teaching career in the town she
           grew up in.

WANGEL   Of course.
           She speaks about you often.

ARNHOLM   She does?

WANGEL   I think it might be good for her...
            To have someone to talk to.
            About the old days.
            We lost a child, you see.

ARNHOLM   I –
            I didn't know that.

WANGEL   Yes.

ARNHOLM   I'm so sorry.

WANGEL   Two and a half years ago now.
            He was only five months.

ARNHOLM   How awful for you both.

WANGEL   She blamed herself, you see.
            I think that's when the trouble started.
            Or, no, perhaps it was before that...
            It's so hard to keep track of...

ARNHOLM   The trouble?

            Pause.

WANGEL   If your wife went down to the water every
            day, without fail, to swim...
            If the prospect of missing this swim became
            a kind of...
            A kind of catastrophe for her...
            What would you make of it?

ARNHOLM   I think I would imagine she enjoyed the
            exertion.

WANGEL   She swims for so long her limbs shake.
            Her teeth chatter.

ARNHOLM   She was always in the water when we were
            friends.
            We could barely coax her out of the sea.

WANGEL   When she comes back to the house she's...
            Different, somehow.

	Closed off…
	I've tried to introduce her to people.
	Encouraged her to make friends.
	But…

ARNHOLM   She won't?

WANGEL   Or can't.

ARNHOLM   Surely not!
          She was always surrounded by friends –

WANGEL   They've got a name for her here.
          They call her 'The Lady from the Sea'.

ELLIDA   (*Off.*) Wangel?

WANGEL   Talk to her, would you?

ARNHOLM   I mean, I'll try –

ELLIDA   (*Off.*) Wangel?
          Are you home?

WANGEL   (*To* ELLIDA.) We're in the arbour.
          (*To* ARNHOLM.) Please.
          It would mean so much to me.
          To us.

ARNHOLM   I'll do whatever I can, of course –

WANGEL   Remind her of when she was the lighthouse
          keeper's daughter.

          ELLIDA *enters, with wet hair and a towel
          around her shoulders.*

          Here she is.
          The mermaid!

ELLIDA   You're here!
          Thank goodness!

WANGEL   Hello, my darling.

ELLIDA   What a wonderful surprise!
          I wasn't expecting you back until this evening.

*She goes to him, kisses him warmly – a little
performatively.*

Keeps a tight hold of his hands.

Now.
You're staying, aren't you?
You aren't rushing back to the surgery?

WANGEL   Not quite yet.

ELLIDA   Oh, close up for the afternoon.
                I've hardly seen you…

WANGEL   Won't you say hello to your old friend?

She turns to ARNHOLM.

ELLIDA   Arnholm?

ARNHOLM   Hello again…!

ELLIDA   Goodness.

She looks at him, taken aback.

ARNHOLM   I hope I'm not completely unrecognisable…!

ELLIDA   No, no, of course, it's just…
                Actually you look exactly the same.

She smiles at him.

They smile at each other.

                And look!
                You're honoured.
                The girls must think the world of you.
                All these flowers!

WANGEL   How was your swim?

ELLIDA   The same.
                It's so cold and dead in that water.
                So dark!
                Like swimming in ink.

WANGEL	We'll be sure not to let the tourist board hire you!
ELLIDA	And then this air is so hot and sticky. Is it as hot and sticky as this in London, Arnholm?
ARNHOLM	It's much worse in London. Noisy too. I forgot how peaceful it is this high up.
ELLIDA	Yes, apart from all these flies buzzing.

WANGEL stands up.

Where are you going?

WANGEL	I have to get back to the surgery, my love.
ELLIDA	So soon? You're not even staying for lunch?
WANGEL	I'll pick something up on my way.
ELLIDA	The girls will be disappointed.
WANGEL	I'll let Bolette know.

He kisses her.

I'm sure you two have lots to catch up on.

ELLIDA	Don't stay too late. Will you?
WANGEL	I promise.

WANGEL exits.

ELLIDA and ARNHOLM are left alone together.

They smile at one another a little awkwardly.

ARNHOLM	What a beautiful view.
ELLIDA	If you climb up that hill you can see the sea. I mean, you can't smell it or hear it but. At least I know it's still there.

They look out in the direction of the distant sea.

This is my arbour.
Wangel had it built for me.

ARNHOLM   Not for both of you?

Beat.

ELLIDA   The girls tend to stay on the veranda.
Wangel goes back and forth between us.

ARNHOLM   Seems sensible.

ELLIDA   We can easily call out to one another.
When we have something to say...

ARNHOLM   If a little lonely.

The sound of music in the distance.

Nearly Carnival.

ELLIDA   It's a strange time of year, isn't it?
I've never liked it.

ARNHOLM   Why?

ELLIDA   That atmosphere.
Can't you feel it?

ARNHOLM   I thought it was supposed to be a celebration.

ELLIDA   But there's that push behind it.
It's forced.
Everyone grinning, singing, drinking, dancing...
If you don't feel like grinning or dancing yourself then...

ARNHOLM   And you don't?

ELLIDA   Oh ignore me!
I'm a little out of sorts today.
That's all.

ARNHOLM   Why's that?

ELLIDA	No particular reason. Perhaps I swam for too long.

Pause.

ARNHOLM	I have to admit, I'm… Surprised. To see you here. Married to the doctor.
ELLIDA	Why? He's a good man. He's a very good man.
ARNHOLM	I don't doubt that for a second.
ELLIDA	So?
ARNHOLM	I just wouldn't have paired him with the lighthouse keeper's daughter.
ELLIDA	Oh. Her…
ARNHOLM	The girl named after a ship. The one they used to call 'The Pagan'.
ELLIDA	We all have to grow up.
ARNHOLM	Is that what this is?
ELLIDA	Have you come here to fight?
ARNHOLM	No.

Pause.

He doesn't know, does he?
How things were left with…
With us?

ELLIDA	How were things left?
ARNHOLM	Come on, Ellida, you know how they were left –
ELLIDA	That's all behind us.

ARNHOLM   Right.
              I see.

ELLIDA   You were my friend.
              My best friend actually.

ARNHOLM   A friend who wanted to be more.

ELLIDA   What do you want me to say?

              Pause.

ARNHOLM   You're right.
              I'm sorry.

ELLIDA   You never wrote.

ARNHOLM   Nor did you.

ELLIDA   Well, no.
              I didn't want to kindle any…

ARNHOLM   No.

ELLIDA   My turn to be sorry.

ARNHOLM   Ah well.
              Can't be helped.

ELLIDA   There must have been others…?
              I mean, it was fifteen years ago.

ARNHOLM   I'm a loyal sort of chap.

ELLIDA   Oh, Arnholm!
              You're still young.
              Go and fall madly in love with someone
              immediately.

ARNHOLM   Bit late for all that, isn't it?
              I'm nearly forty.

ELLIDA   Where's your sense of romance?!

ARNHOLM   Stuck in the past, clearly…

ELLIDA   Oh it's so good to see you!
              To see a friend.
              I'm so glad you're here with us.

ARNHOLM   You don't have many friends up here?

ELLIDA   Oh yes.
            Yes, plenty...
            But no one I can really talk to.

ARNHOLM   You can always talk to me.

            She hesitates.

            Ellida?
            What is it?

ELLIDA   Nothing.

ARNHOLM   There's something.
            I know there is.

ELLIDA   I'm fine.

ARNHOLM   Are you?

ELLIDA   Why wouldn't I be?

ARNHOLM   You tell me.

            She turns away from him.

            Ellida?

ELLIDA   No.
            I can't.

ARNHOLM   You can.

ELLIDA   You wouldn't understand, you...

ARNHOLM   Try me.

ELLIDA   When I told you...
            That we couldn't be together, all those years
            ago.
            I wasn't...
            Completely honest with you.

            ARNHOLM *waits.*

            I couldn't have loved you.
            I couldn't have loved anyone, then.

ARNHOLM	Why not?
ELLIDA	Because I was completely and utterly consumed. With someone else.
ARNHOLM	Who? Not Wangel…
ELLIDA	No. Not Wangel. Years before Wangel.
ARNHOLM	Then who? I can't think of anyone at all who would have –
ELLIDA	It doesn't matter who.
ARNHOLM	But –
ELLIDA	It's enough for you to know that I was… Tangled up in something else. Someone else.
ARNHOLM	And if you hadn't… You might have been able to love – Me? Is that what you're trying to tell me?
ELLIDA	No – !
ARNHOLM	Then what?
ELLIDA	I'm asking you for help, Arnholm!
	Pause.
ARNHOLM	Of course. I'm sorry.
	Pause.
	Does Wangel know? About this… man?
ELLIDA	No. I mean, I told him a version, years ago.

The barest facts.
He doesn't know that I still…

ARNHOLM   Still what?

ELLIDA   What's the matter with me?
Am I ill?
Am I going mad?
Is that what I'm destined for?

ARNHOLM   Of course not.

ELLIDA   But you've never felt like this, have you?
Like something's wormed its way into you
and you can't…
Can't shake it off?

ARNHOLM   Don't be so sure.

ELLIDA   So?
What did you do?

He looks at her.

ARNHOLM   Went to Europe…

*His hand rests on his injured leg for
a moment.*

ELLIDA   Oh, Arnholm.

ARNHOLM   Doesn't matter.

ELLIDA   I really am sorry.

LYNGSTRAND *enters with a bouquet of
flowers.*

LYNGSTRAND Hello?
Hello…?

ELLIDA   Ah.
Mr Lyngstrand, isn't it?

LYNGSTRAND That's me.

ELLIDA   What an impressive bouquet.
I can hardly see you behind it.

LYNGSTRAND   I'm glad you think so.
             They're for you actually.

ELLIDA   For me?

LYNGSTRAND   A humble birthday gift.

ELLIDA   But –

ARNHOLM   It's not your birthday, is it?

LYNGSTRAND   Oh dear...
             I hope it wasn't a secret.

             ELLIDA *looks at him, puzzled.*

             Typical me!
             Always putting my foot in it.
             I should have realised women don't like being
             reminded of things like birthdays.

ELLIDA   Who told you it was my birthday?

LYNGSTRAND   Hilde.

ELLIDA   Hilde?
             Oh.
             Wait.
             She said it was her mother's birthday, did she?

LYNGSTRAND   She didn't say how old you were or anything
             like that.

             ELLIDA *catches* ARNHOLM's *eye.*

ELLIDA   Not at all.
             You're very sweet to bring me flowers.
             And now the cat's out of the bag...
             About my rapidly advancing years...

ARNHOLM   Frankly I'm amazed you're able to stand
             upright.

ELLIDA   In fact, won't you help me into a seat?
             I don't think my ancient legs will hold me up
             much longer...

ARNHOLM *elaborately helps* ELLIDA *into a seat.*

LYNGSTRAND *watches, unsure if he is being made fun of.*

ELLIDA   Oh don't look so worried, Lyngstrand.
              Sit down.
              Join us!

LYNGSTRAND Oh, well, if you're sure...

ELLIDA   You're looking so much better than you did.
              The island must be doing you some good.

LYNGSTRAND Oh yes I'm practically cured.
              This is just a stopover really, on my way to
              New York.
              Thought I'd take advantage of this wonderful
              light.

ELLIDA   This isn't your first time on the island, is it?

LYNGSTRAND No, no.
              I was a sailor on one of the tourist ships for
              a while.
              I had to wear a hat.
              And a kerchief.

ELLIDA   What fun.

LYNGSTRAND It wasn't fun.
              It was horrible.
              I was sick the whole time.

ELLIDA   A sailor without sea legs.
              How unfortunate.

LYNGSTRAND It was my father's idea.
              He practically manhandled me onto the boat
              and sent me on my way.
              He didn't care that I was an artist.

ELLIDA   Surely he meant well.
              Perhaps he hoped you might benefit from the
              freedom of the open seas.

LYNGSTRAND   He was trying to get rid of me.
               It was just after my mother died.
               She knew I was an artist.
               She had an artistic soul.
               Unlike him.
               Ha, he feels terrible now!

ELLIDA   Why's that?

LYNGSTRAND   Because the ship I was on sank!

ELLIDA   It didn't.

LYNGSTRAND   It did!
               We got into the most awful storm and the boat
               didn't stand a chance.
               That's when I got so ill, you see.
               I mean, slightly ill.
               The sea got well and truly into my lungs.
               I practically swallowed the entire ocean.

ELLIDA   How horrible for you.

LYNGSTRAND   Oh no, I was delighted.
               The perfect excuse never to set foot on a ship
               again!
               And it was when I was recovering that I struck
               on the most wonderful idea.

ELLIDA   What idea?

LYNGSTRAND   For my great work of art!
               The one that will ensure I go down in history!

ARNHOLM   Are you an artist?
               I don't think you've mentioned it…

ELLIDA   So it's going to be a painting or – ?

LYNGSTRAND   Oh no.
               No, no, no.
               I have no interest in painting, figurative
               representation, yuck!

ELLIDA   Of course.
               How silly of me.

LYNGSTRAND   It's going to be a sculpture.
Created entirely from found objects.
Stuff I find on the beach.
Bits of old net and shells and seaweed and
dried-up old crabs' claws.
That sort of thing.

ELLIDA   And what will you be making from these
found objects?
Mermaids and mermen?
Ancient sea monsters?

LYNGSTRAND   Let me describe it for you!

He leaps up.

Sets the scene.

Imagine a woman.
Asleep.
Her covers flung off in agitation.
She's dreaming –

ARNHOLM   How will we know she's dreaming?

LYNGSTRAND   The way I fashion it will be very dynamic.
Her face will be expressive of the fact that
she's in the midst of a dream.

ARNHOLM   You'll manage that with some bits of old
claw?

ELLIDA   (*To* ARNHOLM.) Shh.
Go on, Lyngstrand.

LYNGSTRAND   Hovering beside her bed is a figure.
Indistinct.
But clearly a male figure.
Something about the way he's standing
suggests he's both *of* this world.
And *not*.
He's between the two.
Neither alive or dead.

ARNHOLM   What does that mean?

ELLIDA   (*To* ARNHOLM.) Be quiet.

LYNGSTRAND   He is, of course, her husband.
                The husband she betrayed.
                The husband she thought was dead.
                Drowned.
                But he isn't.
                Or perhaps he is.
                Perhaps he's both.

ARNHOLM   He can't be both...!

ELLIDA   Arnholm.
                You're being a philistine.

LYNGSTRAND   The point is he's dragged himself across land
                and sea to find her again.
                Years and years have passed.
                His clothes are torn and his flesh is pulpy and
                his fingernails are blue.
                He's like a monster from the deep.

ELLIDA   So wait.
                He's standing over her?
                While she dreams about him?

LYNGSTRAND   That's exactly right.
                He's both inside her dream and right
                beside her.
                He's two things at once.

ARNHOLM   I still think it's a lot to get across...

LYNGSTRAND   Not at all.
                I'm drawing directly from reality.
                I am channelling the truth.

ARNHOLM   What?

LYNGSTRAND   The man who lurks in the shadows.
                Towering over the bed.
                He was on the ship with me.

                A beat.

ELLIDA   Surely not.

LYNGSTRAND   Oh yes.
                He's the sort of person you don't forget.
                I always knew I'd use him one day.

ELLIDA   So he inspired you.

LYNGSTRAND   I shared a cabin with him for a few weeks.
                He joined us in Jamaica, replaced someone
                who'd been ill.
                He didn't really fit in with the rest of us.

ELLIDA   No?
                Why not?

LYNGSTRAND   He was always teaching himself a new
                language.
                He could speak Chinese, and Greek, and
                Arabic, and Hindi.
                He was teaching himself Norwegian that
                summer.

ELLIDA   Goodness.
                What an enterprising fellow.

LYNGSTRAND   He was always muttering to himself.
                These strange, foreign words...
                Either that or rifling through newspapers.
                Any newspaper he could find, in whatever
                tongue.
                His finger obsessively following the print.

ELLIDA   Whatever can he have been looking for?

LYNGSTRAND   Whatever it was, he found it!

ELLIDA   He did?

LYNGSTRAND   One night.
                The night of the storm.
                He was reading and muttering as usual.
                And then suddenly he let out this great...
                Roar.

	And ripped the newspaper in two. He seemed to be completely convulsed with pain.
ELLIDA	What was wrong? Was he having a fit?
LYNGSTRAND	I thought so, at first. I grabbed him by the shoulders, called his name, tried to get him to focus. Then I heard what he was saying.
ELLIDA	What was he saying?
LYNGSTRAND	It was a kind of incantation.
ELLIDA	How did it go?
LYNGSTRAND	He said – 'She's mine. She's mine. She will always be mine.' *Pause.* And then the storm hit. We were tossed into the sea.
ELLIDA	And what happened to the mysterious man?
LYNGSTRAND	I'm almost certain he drowned.
ELLIDA	Why?
LYNGSTRAND	Only a handful of us were saved. Everyone else…
ELLIDA	Everyone?
LYNGSTRAND	They never did recover all the bodies. But I'd be amazed if any of them got out alive. *Silence.* Anyway! I think I'm going to go and take a dip before my afternoon nap.

I'm sorry again for the…
Indiscretion.

ELLIDA   You're so kind to bring me flowers.
             Thank you.

LYNGSTRAND   And I won't mention a word to anyone else.
             I know it's sensitive.
             For women.
             Goodbye!

             LYNGSTRAND *exits*.

ARNHOLM   (*To* ELLIDA.) You look as if you've seen
             a ghost.

ELLIDA   What?

ARNHOLM   I know it must be horribly painful.
             But it can't have come as too much of a shock.
             Can it?

ELLIDA   You're right.
             I suppose I always knew, in a way.

ARNHOLM   Knew what?

ELLIDA   That he'd come back.

ARNHOLM   But –
             It can't be that boy's mad seafaring tale that
             has upset you!

ELLIDA   What exactly was mad about it?

ARNHOLM   Well, it's pure melodrama!
             'She will always be mine'!

             ARNHOLM *laughs*.

             After a moment, ELLIDA *joins in*.

             They laugh together, ELLIDA *with a hint of
             desperation*.

             Then she stops.

             I assumed you were upset because, well…

He gestures to the flowers.

You must know they don't mean to exclude you.
It's natural they want to remember her…

ELLIDA   My husband celebrating the memory of his first wife doesn't upset me in the slightest.

ARNHOLM   But I suppose it's never nice to be reminded, is it?
That we aren't the first…

ELLIDA   I don't own Wangel.
He has a past.
Just as I do.

ARNHOLM   It's all very well to have a past.
As long as it stays there.

WANGEL, HILDE *and* BOLETTE *enter.*

HILDE   Ugh.
Who brought that hideous bunch of flowers?

ELLIDA   It was your friend.
Mr Lyngstrand.

HILDE   He's not *my* friend.

BOLETTE   Lyngstrand was here?

ARNHOLM   Count your blessings you missed him…

ELLIDA   He very kindly wanted to celebrate my birthday.

WANGEL   Your birthday?

HILDE   I didn't say anything, it wasn't me!

WANGEL   Oh, Ellida, I'm sorry –

ELLIDA   Come on.
Let's get these in some water before they wilt.
Will someone help me find a vase?

WANGEL   I tried to talk to the girls, but...

ELLIDA   You don't have to keep the celebrations
             a secret from me.
             Why can't I join in?

WANGEL   Would you like to?

ELLIDA   Yes.
             Why not?

HILDE   (*To* BOLETTE.) Listen to her, sucking up to
             Dad.

BOLETTE   You always think the worst of her.

WANGEL   Ellida –

             ELLIDA *takes his arm.*

ELLIDA   Come on.
             Let's open some champagne.
             We're celebrating!

ACT TWO

HILDE *and* BOLETTE *have just arrived at the top of The Heights*.

BOLETTE *is out of breath*.

HILDE	Come on, slowcoach!
BOLETTE	Why do we have to go so fast?
HILDE	I couldn't stand another second of that awful boring Lyngstrand. He's so full of himself. And with absolutely nothing to back it up.
BOLETTE	Then why are you always badgering him?
HILDE	I'm not.
BOLETTE	Yes you are.
HILDE	Look at him! Don't you think it's funny to see him panting along like that?
BOLETTE	No. It just makes me feel sorry for him.
HILDE	Exactly. Because he's tragic. He is tragedy incarnate.
BOLETTE	And why exactly is that funny?
HILDE	You have to laugh. Otherwise you'd just weep…
	LYNGSTRAND *enters, out of breath*.
LYNGSTRAND	Oof! That wasn't nearly as steep as you said it would be.

HILDE   You're probably much fitter than us.

LYNGSTRAND Yes I expect so.

HILDE   Will you come dancing with us tonight?

LYNGSTRAND I could, I suppose.

HILDE   Are you a good dancer?

LYNGSTRAND I haven't had much cause for dancing.

HILDE   Because of your poor chest?

LYNGSTRAND Well...
                 My work keeps me very, very busy.

HILDE   Of course.
                 Your terribly important work.

LYNGSTRAND Will you be coming dancing, Bolette?

BOLETTE   I don't know.
                 Maybe.

HILDE   What a relief it must be for you.
                 Looking so much healthier every day.
                 Almost offensively healthy, in fact.

LYNGSTRAND Oh yes.
                 I'll be leaving for New York in no time.

HILDE   How exciting.

LYNGSTRAND The gallery have been writing actually,
                 begging me to arrive as soon as I possibly can.
                 I'm just creating a bit of suspense.
                 Mystique.

HILDE   That's very sensible of you.
                 I'd do the same.

LYNGSTRAND (*To* BOLETTE.) What's this you're making?

BOLETTE   A garland.
                 I always make them...

LYNGSTRAND What flower is that?

BOLETTE   This one?
                Hibiscus.

                She hangs the garland around
                LYNGSTRAND*'s neck.*

                He looks up at her eagerly.

                She laughs.

                HILDE *watches them.*

HILDE   All this adversity.
                And yet you keep going.

LYNGSTRAND   You have to.
                There's no use dwelling on the difficult times.
                You have to look forward.

HILDE   What an inspiring motto.

BOLETTE   Oh look.
                They're all about to take the wrong path.

LYNGSTRAND   Shall I run and intercept them?

HILDE   Yes, run, Hans, run!

BOLETTE   Don't hurt yourself – !

LYNGSTRAND   Downhill is easy!

                LYNGSTRAND *sets off at a trot.*

                HILDE *and* BOLETTE *watch him.*

HILDE   Would you kiss him?

BOLETTE   What?

HILDE   I would.
                He'd definitely kiss me back.
                Do you think he'd use his tongue?
                Or would he be all thin-lipped and pecky, like
                a beaky bird.
                God, I bet he would.

BOLETTE   He doesn't see you like that.

HILDE	It's not like I'm interested in him. He's poor as a church mouse. All this talk of New York and galleries. It's embarrassing.
BOLETTE	So why kiss him if he's so pathetic?
HILDE	Because of the dying thing, of course.
BOLETTE	What?
HILDE	Imagine. Kissing someone you knew would be dead in five… Three… Maybe even one year's time!
BOLETTE	You're horrible.
HILDE	Like kissing a corpse. Am I thinner than I was yesterday?
BOLETTE	Not this again.
HILDE	You eat too much. It weighs you down. If you stopped you might actually *do* something instead of just talking about it.
BOLETTE	And anyway, he's not dying.
HILDE	Yes he is. Dad says.
BOLETTE	Really?
HILDE	He'll be lucky if he makes it to thirty.
BOLETTE	God. Poor thing…
HILDE	Do you like him?
BOLETTE	No.
HILDE	I think you do. I suppose he's slightly better than that old man who used to teach you.

BOLETTE	Arnholm's not old. He's only thirty-something.
HILDE	Nearly forty.
BOLETTE	The same age as The Lady from the Sea.
HILDE	I wouldn't be surprised if there was something going on between them.
BOLETTE	What?
HILDE	Look at them. She's barely glanced at Dad all day. She's just whispering with Arnholm all the time.

They look.

Do you think she's going mad?

BOLETTE	Who?
HILDE	Our stepmother.
BOLETTE	No.
HILDE	Her mother went mad.
BOLETTE	You don't know that.
HILDE	She threw herself into the sea.
BOLETTE	Doesn't mean she was mad. Sad, maybe...
HILDE	Are you sad?
BOLETTE	What?
HILDE	I am sometimes.

Pause.

BOLETTE	Hilde...

ELLIDA, ARNHOLM, WANGEL *and* LYNGSTRAND *enter.*

ELLIDA   Look!
            This is what I mean!
            You climb all the way to the top...
            You're longing to catch a glimpse of the sea
            and –
            All these trees are in the way!

ARNHOLM   It's still a pretty remarkable view.

BOLETTE   It's better on the other side.

WANGEL   You're right.
            It's a bit more of a walk but there's still time.
            What do you say, Ellida?

ELLIDA   You go.
            I'm going to sit here for a while.

WANGEL   In that case, I'll stay as well...

HILDE   Oh, Dad – !

WANGEL   We'll meet you back at the house for dinner.

BOLETTE   Would you like to see the other view,
            Arnholm?

ARNHOLM   Yes very much.

LYNGSTRAND I would too!

HILDE   The path only takes two at a time.
            You can walk with me.

LYNGSTRAND Oh.
            All right.

HILDE   But don't stand so close.
            People will think you're my suitor.

ARNHOLM   Would you like to walk with me, Bolette?

BOLETTE   Um.

            She glances at LYNGSTRAND *for a second.*

            Yes all right.

LYNGSTRAND, HILDE, BOLETTE *and* ARNHOLM *exit.*

WANGEL *and* ELLIDA *are alone.*

They look at each other, smile, a little embarrassed.

WANGEL   Feels like a while since we've been alone together.
              Doesn't it?

ELLIDA   Come and sit next to me then.

              After a moment, WANGEL *sits next to her.*

WANGEL   We should talk.

ELLIDA   Should we?
              What about?

WANGEL   This.
              Us.

ELLIDA   Us?

WANGEL   We can't go on like this!

              Pause.

              He takes her hand.

              Can we be honest with one another?

ELLIDA   Of course.
              Aren't we always?

WANGEL   Once, perhaps.
              Now...

ELLIDA   I haven't intended to keep anything from you.

WANGEL   Perhaps not.
              But you have, all the same.

ELLIDA   Have I?

WANGEL   I apologise for not realising sooner.
              I've been short-sighted.
              I'm sorry.

ELLIDA	What exactly have you realised?
WANGEL	Well, that… That you're uncomfortable being a man's second wife.

Pause.

ELLIDA	I see.
WANGEL	You think she casts a shadow over you. Over us.
ELLIDA	Do I?
WANGEL	I can't pretend she didn't exist. That I didn't, at one time, love her very much. That would be doing both of you a disservice.
ELLIDA	Wangel –
WANGEL	But let me reassure you that I'm completely, utterly focused on you. There isn't any kind of spectre here. I'm yours. Entirely.
ELLIDA	As I'm yours.
WANGEL	And that's why you haven't felt able to…

She waits.

To share a bed with me these past months.

She turns away from him.

ELLIDA	So. This is your diagnosis…
WANGEL	Will you allow me to suggest a remedy?
ELLIDA	Go on.
WANGEL	We move. Start afresh.
ELLIDA	Move?

WANGEL	I know you find it hard, all the way up here. The house shrouded in trees... You're always saying you wish there was more light.
ELLIDA	No. This is your home. Our home...
WANGEL	But you miss it. Don't you? The lighthouse. The sea.
ELLIDA	Yes. I'm homesick for the sea... I wish I could smell it, hear it. But –
WANGEL	Then why not let me move us back there? Isn't that the simplest solution?
ELLIDA	Your whole life is here. Your business...
WANGEL	Maybe it's time I wound that down a little.
ELLIDA	But...
WANGEL	Maybe I should be spending more time with you? If that's what you'd like?
ELLIDA	I –
WANGEL	I've been spending too much time at the surgery. I know I have. That stops, as of now.
ELLIDA	Wangel –
WANGEL	I'll be as available as you want, Ellida. Our marriage is the most important thing here.

And I'll devote myself to you, if that's what
you want.

Pause.

Is that what you want...?

ELLIDA   I don't want you to change anything.
            For me.
            That isn't right.
            Or fair...

WANGEL   But we have to at least try –

ELLIDA   No.
            I can't let you.

WANGEL   Why not?

ELLIDA   Because...
            Because what if we do and...

WANGEL   And?

ELLIDA   It doesn't help.

            Pause.

            What then, Wangel?
            All that upheaval.
            And to no end.

WANGEL   But –

ELLIDA   You and the girls uprooted for nothing.
            And me...
            Still feeling like...

WANGEL   Like what?
            I wish you'd talk to me, Ellida.

ELLIDA   I'm trying...

WANGEL   I'll do anything.
            I'll do whatever it takes.

ELLIDA   This isn't for you to fix.

WANGEL   Then what...
             What can I do...?

             ELLIDA *takes a deep breath*.

ELLIDA   You're right.
             You asked for honesty, and honesty is what
             you deserve.
             Very well.

             She takes his hands.

             Do you remember...
             In those days after my father died.
             You kept on visiting me.
             Always with some new excuse even though
             your duties as a doctor were clearly past...

WANGEL   Was I really so transparent?

ELLIDA   That night when...
             When you found me at the water's edge.
             I almost couldn't speak because of the pain.

WANGEL   I remember.

ELLIDA   You told me about her.
             Your wife.
             How she'd withered away in front of you.
             How you couldn't save her.

WANGEL   Yes...

ELLIDA   You said –
             I know how this feels.
             I know the way it closes up your throat when
             all you want to do is scream.
             For the first time, someone was telling me
             the truth.
             You weren't afraid to voice the horror of death.

             They squeeze one another's hands.

             I told you something in return.
             That there was someone in my past too.

Someone I loved.
And who I'd lost.

WANGEL   I know what you're about to tell me.

ELLIDA   Do you?

WANGEL   Arnholm.

She stares at him.

ELLIDA   No.
Not him.

WANGEL   Then who?

Pause.

ELLIDA   I was sixteen.
Just after my mother died.
A ship came to the port to be repaired.
The *Lorelei*.

WANGEL   I remember that ship.
The captain was murdered.
They found him in his cabin with a hole in the
middle of him.

ELLIDA   Yes.

WANGEL   I was there when they did the autopsy.
He'd been gouged straight through.
They said it was the second mate who did it.
That he stabbed the captain, then drowned
himself.

ELLIDA   He didn't drown himself.
He went north.

WANGEL   How do you – ?

ELLIDA   Because he told me.
The man I loved was the second mate.

Pause.

WANGEL	But – A murderer, Ellida?!
ELLIDA	He told me he had to do it.
WANGEL	And you believed him?
ELLIDA	Yes.
WANGEL	Why?
ELLIDA	I had to.
WANGEL	Almost a total stranger –
ELLIDA	He didn't feel like a stranger. Not then.
WANGEL	Did you even know his name?
ELLIDA	He said he was called Alfred Johnson. But sometimes he gave himself a different name. Friman. He was a boy. Almost a man…
WANGEL	A boy? Capable of such brutality?
ELLIDA	But he wasn't brutal. Not with me. We swam together every day for a week. It was so hot, that water, it almost burned you. He made me put my face under it and open my eyes and there was a whole world there. Then he made me lie on my back and look at the sky. There was a whole world there too. For one whole week he was all I breathed…
WANGEL	But Ellida – !
ELLIDA	Then one morning, the last morning… He came to me.

Said he had to leave the next day.
We had a matter of hours left together.
There was blood on his shirt.
It stained my dress...

She closes her eyes for a moment.

Takes a deep breath.

WANGEL   And then he ran off into obscurity?

ELLIDA   Yes.
But not before we made our promise.

WANGEL   What promise?

ELLIDA   He wore a ring on his finger.
He took it off, then pointed to the one I wore.
The one my mother gave me, before she...
He took a piece of string and threaded the
rings onto it.
His ring, and mine.
He made me kiss them.
Then he threw them into the water.
Said, now we are married to the sea...
We are sworn to one another forever.
The sea will carry our vow for eternity.
You know, don't you, how much that means
on this island?

WANGEL   I –

ELLIDA   By the time the sun was up, he was gone.
It was like a curse was lifted.
I could breathe again!
I wrote to him.
Straight away.
I said that what we'd had was madness and
we both had to forget it.
Forget our promise to the sea.
Let it go.

WANGEL   Of course.

ELLIDA   He wrote back.
                It was as if he hadn't read a word I'd written.
                He just told me he would return for me.
                That I was to wait.

WANGEL   Wait?

ELLIDA   I wrote again, of course.
                Said that I couldn't wait for him.
                Couldn't be the kind of woman who sits and
                pines.
                He wrote again.
                He wrote many times.
                For a whole year.
                From China, Australia, India, America.
                Just kept saying that he would come back.
                That I must wait for him.
                And I kept writing, saying, no, no.
                I won't wait for you.
                I can't.
                And then it was as if he finally heard me.
                I sent him a letter, the day before my
                seventeenth birthday and...
                He never replied.
                It was like he just evaporated.

WANGEL   So.
                So, then, it's over.
                He heard you.
                He got the message.

ELLIDA   No.
                It isn't over.
                I don't know if it will ever be over.

WANGEL   But this is – !
                We're talking about something that happened
                years and years ago!
                It's madness to keep –

ELLIDA   It was over.
                For a time.
                Then it was as if he came back.

WANGEL	Came back?
ELLIDA	He knew where I was. He found me. He crept into our bedroom while I slept.
WANGEL	You mean… A dream?
ELLIDA	Yes. No.
WANGEL	My darling. Of course it was a dream.
ELLIDA	Every night since. It began three years ago. When I was expecting our son.
WANGEL	My love. Isn't it sensible to maybe…? To perhaps explain this as something that came about because… Because of what you were going through at that time?
ELLIDA	No –
WANGEL	It's so normal. So many women go through this. Pregnancy is such an extreme experience. It's natural that it takes a toll on the mind as well as –
ELLIDA	If you carry on like this I'll scream, I swear.

Silence.

WANGEL	So he's been there. In our room, with us. For three years?
ELLIDA	Yes.

WANGEL	I had no idea. All this time and you've… You've loved someone else.
ELLIDA	No. I've only loved you.
WANGEL	You tell me you love someone else. Then you tell me you love only me. Which is it?
ELLIDA	Wangel –
WANGEL	You can understand my confusion.
ELLIDA	Can't you see? I don't want to feel like this! I want you to take your surgeon's knife and slice it clean out of me.
WANGEL	But this isn't something you can just – !
ELLIDA	Then what is it? What is this thing I'm feeling, Wangel? What?
WANGEL	If we move it will fade, I'm sure of it!
ELLIDA	No. It would follow me. The fear…
WANGEL	But what are you afraid of?
ELLIDA	Him.
WANGEL	He can't hurt you. He's probably on the other side of the world. He's probably dead, Ellida –
	HILDE, LYNGSTRAND, ARNHOLM *and* BOLETTE *enter.*
HILDE	Dinner's cancelled. We're all going dancing instead.

BOLETTE	We thought we'd come and collect you.
WANGEL	I'm… I'm not sure if we'll be joining you. I'm sorry.
LYNGSTRAND	I need to go back and change.
HILDE	What will you wear? Will you wear shorts?
LYNGSTRAND	I never wear shorts unless I absolutely have to.
ELLIDA	Lyngstrand, wait a moment.

LYNGSTRAND *turns to* ELLIDA.

You're going dancing?

LYNGSTRAND	Apparently so.
HILDE	I'm going to change too. I'm going to put on my most ravishing dress!
LYNGSTRAND	What will you wear, Bolette?
BOLETTE	Just this, I expect.
HILDE	What? That?
BOLETTE	What's wrong with it?
HILDE	I don't even know where to start.
ELLIDA	(*To* LYNGSTRAND.) But is your health up to it? Dancing?
LYNGSTRAND	Oh I should think so.
ELLIDA	But it's only been… Let me see. How long has it been since the shipwreck that made you so ill?
LYNGSTRAND	About three years, more or less.
WANGEL	Three years?

LYNGSTRAND	Yes I think that's right. Yes I'm sure it is. We left America in June. Then hit some squally weather in July. That's what did for us.
BOLETTE	Dad? Are you coming?
WANGEL	I... What?
BOLETTE	It would do you good to dance... I can teach you how to waltz.
HILDE	'To waltz.' Are you fifty-seven?
BOLETTE	Please, Dad. I so want you to see the lights down at the Marina. It's beautiful at the moment, with the Carnival decorations going up –
WANGEL	Not now, Bolette.
BOLETTE	But –
WANGEL	Not now.

Stung, BOLETTE *exits.*

ARNHOLM	Bolette, wait...

ARNHOLM *goes after her.*

HILDE	Come on, Hans. I'm going to teach you how to dance the way we like to here. And I absolutely promise you it won't be a waltz.

HILDE *seizes* LYNGSTRAND's *hand and drags him off.*

WANGEL *and* ELLIDA *are alone again.*

ELLIDA   He was on that boat.
            I'm sure of it.
            Friman.
            Alfred Johnson.
            Whatever he calls himself.

WANGEL   I see.
            So you believe in fairytales now?
            In sailor boys who come back from the dead?

ELLIDA   He found out I'd married you on board that
            ship.
            That I was expecting your child.
            I know it.

WANGEL   This can't be the thing that pulls us apart,
            Ellida.
            It's too strange, it's...
            It's too dark.

ELLIDA   Ever since that moment.
            Every time I close my eyes...
            His face is always in shadow.
            But I can feel him there.

WANGEL   Let's go back to the house.
            Come on.

ELLIDA   He used to wear a pin on his shirt.
            A pearl.
            Like the big, cold eye of a fish.
            A dead fish.
            The pearl is the only thing I can see when he
            stands there.

WANGEL   It's a dream, Ellida.
            It's only a dream.

ELLIDA   When I looked into our son's eyes.
            I saw that pearl.

WANGEL   Don't bring him into this –

ELLIDA   I was afraid of him, Wangel.

WANGEL   No.
          You weren't.

ELLIDA   Sometimes his eyes were bright and alive.
          Like when the sun shines on the sea.
          I felt like I might be able to love him then.

WANGEL   You did love him.
          You did.

ELLIDA   And sometimes they were flat and grey and
          cold like the lagoon.
          I couldn't see anything in them.
          Nothing at all.

WANGEL   You loved your son.

ELLIDA   He had his eyes, Wangel.
          He had the Stranger's eyes.

          Silence.

          Now do you see why I can't sleep in that bed
          next to you?

          She turns and exits.

WANGEL   Ellida.
          Ellida, wait –

ACT THREE

The bottom of WANGEL*'s garden.*

There is an ornamental pond.

HILDE *is on her stomach, peering into it.*

BOLETTE *sits nearby, with books beside her.*

LYNGSTRAND *watches* HILDE.

HILDE *plunges her hands into the water.*

HILDE	There!
LYNGSTRAND	You can't catch them.
HILDE	I can. I nearly did just then.
LYNGSTRAND	Carp are such ugly fish, aren't they?
HILDE	They're hideous. And huge. They're far too big for this dank little pond.
BOLETTE	Leave them alone, Hilde.
HILDE	I'm going to scoop them all up and carry them to the shore in a bucket. Then I'm going to fling them into the waves and watch them swim away. To freedom.
BOLETTE	They couldn't survive in the sea. They're freshwater fish.
HILDE	What, really?
BOLETTE	Mum and Dad had them imported from Europe.

	They're older than us. They should have just let them be really. It's cruel.
HILDE	In that case I'm going to put them out of their misery.
LYNGSTRAND	How?
HILDE	I'm going to bash each of them on the head with a big stone.
LYNGSTRAND	Oh just leave them be. They don't know any different.
HILDE	Poor stupid blind fish.

ARNHOLM enters.

ARNHOLM	What are you three up to?
HILDE	Fishing.
ARNHOLM	Seems an odd place to fish. There's a whole ocean out there!
HILDE	They're slithering round to the other side now. Look. Let's follow them. Coming?
LYNGSTRAND	Yes, all right.
BOLETTE	Don't do anything to the fish, Hilde. Promise?
HILDE	No.

LYNGSTRAND and HILDE exit.

ARNHOLM smiles at BOLETTE.

She smiles back, then looks back at her book.

Silence.

ARNHOLM	What are you reading?

BOLETTE	Take your pick. I've got three on the go at the moment.
	He peers at the books.
ARNHOLM	You're interested in botany, are you?
BOLETTE	I'm interested in lots of things.
ARNHOLM	I'm glad to see you haven't changed.
BOLETTE	Haven't I?
ARNHOLM	You were always reading. Every spare second you had. You once boasted you read three books in a week. Do you still manage that?
BOLETTE	Sometimes. When there's time.
ARNHOLM	You're busy here?
	Pause.
BOLETTE	Perhaps it looks like the height of idleness. But there's a lot to do.
ARNHOLM	I don't doubt it.
BOLETTE	I do most of the housekeeping here.
ARNHOLM	On your own?
BOLETTE	After Mother died, I... Got into the habit of it.
ARNHOLM	Is it still your responsibility?
BOLETTE	No one else does it if I don't.
ARNHOLM	Not even Ellida?
BOLETTE	No.
	Pause.
ARNHOLM	But you still read when you get the chance.

BOLETTE	Of course. It's the only way I get to actually experience life. In any real sense.
ARNHOLM	Here doesn't feel like life?
BOLETTE	It feels like paradise.
ARNHOLM	Doesn't sound so bad...
BOLETTE	Paradise is all well and good. But not when you're trapped in it.
ARNHOLM	Are you trapped?
BOLETTE	We're not so different from the carp in that pond. Whole shoals of fish swimming in a vast ocean nearby. A vast ocean they know nothing about... Hilde's right. We should set them free.
ARNHOLM	The sea would kill them.
BOLETTE	But at least they'd have tasted it for a moment... Freedom... Wouldn't that make it worth it?
ARNHOLM	Paradise doesn't have to be a trap. Think of all the people who flock into the capital.
BOLETTE	Oh they flock *in* all right. But then they flock right on out again.
ARNHOLM	Ah.
BOLETTE	We're the ones left behind. We're the ones who have to live in it.
ARNHOLM	So what's it like? Living in it?

BOLETTE	Well... Each activity happens at its allotted time.
ARNHOLM	What sort of activities?
BOLETTE	I'm almost embarrassed to tell you.
ARNHOLM	Go on.
BOLETTE	Bridge is on Mondays. Tea with the governor's wife on Tuesdays. We go to the hairdresser's on Wednesdays.
ARNHOLM	And what do you ask for?
BOLETTE	If I'm feeling really daring I might ask for a wave. With a blonde rinse.
ARNHOLM	How thrilling.
BOLETTE	See. I knew you were laughing at me.
ARNHOLM	I'm not, I promise! But do you have to do all those things? Couldn't you do something else?
BOLETTE	Like what?
ARNHOLM	Well, like what you really want to do? *Pause.*
BOLETTE	But that's impossible.
ARNHOLM	Why?
BOLETTE	Because it's... No. It's too much.
ARNHOLM	Go on. Tell me what you crave more than anything in the world.
BOLETTE	You really want to know?

ARNHOLM   I'm asking, aren't I?

She considers him.

BOLETTE   All right then.
               I want to know something about everything.

ARNHOLM   Aha.
               Knowledge.

BOLETTE   More than that.
               Education.

ARNHOLM   Forgive me if I'm speaking out of turn, but...
               Did you never have any plans to perhaps...
               Go to university?
               You've always been so bright.

Pause.

BOLETTE   I can't leave Dad.

ARNHOLM   Your dad's got Ellida.

BOLETTE   Does he?

They look at each other.

               Anyway she –
               She doesn't notice anything...
               She's so wrapped up in herself.
               Maybe it's the pills...

ARNHOLM   What pills?

Pause.

BOLETTE   The point is, she doesn't understand what he
               needs.
               Not really.

ARNHOLM   What does he need?

BOLETTE   He needs to be looked after, he...!
               I have to be around all the time otherwise I'm
               worried he'll...!

ARNHOLM   What?

BOLETTE   It doesn't matter.

ARNHOLM   Tell me.

BOLETTE   He has this horrible, false, forced kind of…
Cheerfulness.
He wants everyone to be happy all the time.
But he's not happy…
If he was happy, then he wouldn't…
Ellida doesn't have a clue.

ARNHOLM   About what?

BOLETTE   You must have noticed.

ARNHOLM   I'm not sure.

BOLETTE   He's good at hiding it.
But not that good.

Pause.

ARNHOLM   But.
That shouldn't be a reason for you to sacrifice your future.

BOLETTE   I love him.

ARNHOLM   So does Hilde.
So does Ellida –

BOLETTE   But I'm the only one who really understands him.
If I go then he'll just…
I feel too guilty.

ARNHOLM   He's a grown man.

BOLETTE   He's fragile.
You don't realise…

ARNHOLM   Your future is in your hands.
You don't have to be like the carp.

BOLETTE *closes her book.*

BOLETTE   What do you do about guilt?

ARNHOLM   You've got nothing to feel guilty about.

BOLETTE   Then why do I feel it?
             All the time?

ARNHOLM   Perhaps we get it mixed up with love.

             Pause.

BOLETTE   You're right.
             I know you're right.

ARNHOLM   I just don't want to see you waste your
             talents.

BOLETTE   Will you talk to him?

ARNHOLM   Me?

BOLETTE   Tell him that I...
             That you can see potential in me.
             That you can see it would do me the world of
             good to get away and –

ARNHOLM   Do you really need his permission?

BOLETTE   Please.
             Will you?

ARNHOLM   Of course.
             If you think it really matters, then...

BOLETTE   He likes you so much.
             He listens to you.

ARNHOLM   I just want you to realise that you have a say
             in this.

BOLETTE   Do I?

ARNHOLM   Of course!
             You're an adult!

BOLETTE   No one's ever called me an adult before.
             Feels funny...

ELLIDA *enters, wearing a hat.*

ELLIDA   Here you both are!
            What a glorious day.
            Isn't it?
            I've been out walking with Wangel.
            A lovely long walk in the rainforest.
            I feel a million times better!

ARNHOLM   Come and join us on the lawn.

ELLIDA   No, no, I won't.
            Wangel and I are off sailing soon.
            On the lakes.
            Where is he?
            He said he'd only be a moment.
            Oh it was beautiful in the rainforest today.
            Everything feels so much fresher, don't you
            think?

BOLETTE   There'll be a storm later.

ELLIDA   A storm?
            No!
            Look at that sky!
            There's not a cloud to be seen.

BOLETTE   There will be.
            You mark my words.

ELLIDA   How can you sit there looking so lazy!?
            Come on.
            Let's do something.

BOLETTE   I thought you said you were going sailing.

ELLIDA   Tomorrow then.
            What are you doing tomorrow?
            We could go and pick some fruit for lunch.

BOLETTE   I'm going to the market for that.

ELLIDA   I'll come with you.
            We'll go and speak to the shopkeepers and
            make friends.

We'll invite them here.
We could have a party!
What do you say?

BOLETTE   Maybe.

ELLIDA   Look at this sunset.
                 Have you ever seen anything like it?
                 We really do live in paradise.
                 Don't we, Bolette?

                 She looks out to the lagoon.

                 Goodness.
                 Whose yacht is that?

BOLETTE   Oh that one.
                 It belongs to The Hollywood Actor.

ARNHOLM   It's enormous.
                 Does it normally stop here?

BOLETTE   About once a year.
                 You look up and, suddenly, it's there.
                 Dwarfing everything else.

ARNHOLM   It's certainly ostentatious.

BOLETTE   The crew scurry over it like lizards, getting
                 it ready.
                 Then The Actor descends in his helicopter.
                 With a different woman every time.
                 They disappear inside and then, several hours
                 later, they emerge.
                 Gorge themselves on champagne and lobster
                 in the Marina.
                 Or he does anyway.
                 The woman never eats anything.
                 Then a few days later you look up and it's
                 vanished.
                 As if it never was.

ELLIDA   I'd like to be like him.

ARNHOLM   What?
             Dining with mystery women every night?

ELLIDA   Constantly on the water.
             Shifting from port to port.
             That's the way to live.

ARNHOLM   In light of my journey here, I'd have to
             disagree with you.

ELLIDA   But motion is good for us!
             It's unpredictable.
             It keeps us alive.

ARNHOLM   Or makes us ill.

ELLIDA   No, Arnholm!
             We've got it all wrong.
             We've marooned ourselves on land.
             We should have made the sea our home.

ARNHOLM   The sea's all well and good for whales and
             dolphins.
             Not for us.

ELLIDA   But the sea could be our cure.
             I think that explains it actually.

ARNHOLM   Explains what?

ELLIDA   Why we all feel so miserable all the time.
             So restless.

ARNHOLM   All of us?

ELLIDA   There's always a storm coming.
             Summer never lasts.

ARNHOLM   It's not over yet.

ELLIDA   It's like the water on the lagoon, there, see?
             It looks like silver, doesn't it?
             With the sun on it.
             Like a mirror.
             But then tomorrow, or the day after...

The sun will go behind a cloud and in an
instant it will be dark and...

BOLETTE *and* ARNHOLM *exchange
a glance.*

I'm sorry!
I always get a bit maudlin at the end of the
season.
Lots of people do.
What on earth is Wangel doing?!
Arnholm, would you go and chivvy him
for me?

ARNHOLM   I can try –

ELLIDA   When I don't see his face, you see...
I forget what he looks like.
Isn't that strange?
That's why I need him close to me, all the
time.
Because otherwise I forget...
Now.
Bolette.
Who do you want to invite to the party?

BOLETTE   I don't want a party.

ELLIDA   Come on.
Why don't you put your books down for
a minute?
We really should make a contribution to the
festivities this year.
Let's make a list of all the people to invite.

BOLETTE   I hate parties.
I've always hated them.

ARNHOLM   Bolette –

BOLETTE   And I don't want to put my books down.
My books are the only thing I'm actually
interested in.

ELLIDA   I –
          I'm sorry.

ARNHOLM   Bolette, let's go and see if we can find your
          father…

BOLETTE   I know where he is.
          He'll be down at the Marina waiting for the
          yacht to come in.
          He'll be wanting to go to the bar.

          BOLETTE *exits*.

ELLIDA   Bolette…?

ARNHOLM   It's all right.
          She'll simmer down soon.

ELLIDA   I've embarrassed myself.
          Haven't I?

ARNHOLM   Forget about it.

ELLIDA   What was I trying to prove?
          That I'm just a young girl, like she is?

ARNHOLM   Don't worry.
          I'll talk to her.

          ARNHOLM *exits*.

          ELLIDA *is alone*.

          She looks around her.

          She peers into the pond.

          Looks at her reflection.

          She puts her hand up to her face.

          She touches it.

          *The sound of a storm, distant and low, begins
          to rumble.*

          ELLIDA *keeps touching her face.*

THE STRANGER *appears at the fence, behind* ELLIDA.

She cannot see him yet.

STRANGER   Ellida.

A long pause.

Slowly, ELLIDA *turns to face him.*

They stare at each other.

ELLIDA   It's you.

They stare at each other.

She starts to smile.

You came back.

STRANGER   Yes.

ELLIDA   It's actually you...

THE STRANGER *takes a step closer.*

ELLIDA *takes a step back.*

Who are you?

STRANGER   You know who I am.

ELLIDA   No I don't.
I don't know anything about you.

STRANGER   I promised.
That I would come back for you.

ELLIDA   Twenty years ago.
Twenty years ago you said that.

STRANGER   I've been trying to make my way to you.
All these years I've been trying.

ELLIDA   You're...
You're too late.

STRANGER   I've been all over the world, Ellida.
Trying to find my way back.

ELLIDA   Look around you.
                This is my home now.
                This is where I belong.

STRANGER   I've made my bed in crates of fish.
                In ship kitchens and dockyards and in the
                bowels of the schooners of the rich.
                I've been doing it for twenty years.
                All because of you.

                He starts to climb over the fence.

ELLIDA   You can't come in here.
                Don't.
                If you come any closer I'll scream.

                He stands in front of her.

                No fence between them any more.

                You smell of the sea.

STRANGER   I've come to take you away from here.

ELLIDA   God, your eyes...

                She stares into THE STRANGER*'s eyes.*

                Where will you take me?

STRANGER   Wherever the tide takes us.

ELLIDA   Seeing you again...

                She smiles, still staring into his eyes.

                She reaches up to touch his face.

                Then she stops herself, turns away.

                Shields her eyes.

                I can't.

STRANGER   Yes.
                You can.

ELLIDA   No.

STRANGER   Why won't you look at me, Ellida?

*She shows him her wedding ring, still not
looking into his eyes.*

ELLIDA   Look.

STRANGER   But that means nothing.

ELLIDA   Not to him…

STRANGER   We threw ours into the sea.

ELLIDA   Yes.
              When I was a girl.

STRANGER   You're still that girl.
              I see her.
              I see you.

ELLIDA   No.

STRANGER   Remember when I buried you in the sand.
              Gave you that mermaid's tale.

ELLIDA   No…

STRANGER   Then I brushed the sand off your body.
              By the time I got to your skin you were
              shaking…

ELLIDA   Why did you take so long to come to me?
              Why, why, why?

              She pushes THE STRANGER *in the chest.*

              And again.

              Again and again.

              *Then she wraps her arms around him, her
              face against his chest.*

              Oh God, I remember it now…

              He strokes her hair.

              She disentangles herself from his embrace.

              The horror.

              WANGEL *enters.*

He stares at THE STRANGER *and* ELLIDA.

WANGEL   (*To* THE STRANGER.) Who the hell are you?

ELLIDA *turns and runs to* WANGEL.

She buries her head in his chest.

Who is this man?
What has he done to you?

ELLIDA   Don't let me look at him.

STRANGER   Ellida –

WANGEL   How dare you say her name!

ELLIDA   Don't let me turn round.
Don't let me look into his eyes.

WANGEL   You don't know this man, do you?

ELLIDA   Yes.
I know him.

WANGEL   What does he want?
(*To* THE STRANGER.) What do you want?

STRANGER   Ask her.
She'll tell you.

WANGEL   (*To* THE STRANGER.) You'll state your
purpose here to me.

He waits.

Very well.
If you won't…
I'm going to have to ask you to get out.
Immediately.

STRANGER   I'll leave when I choose.
Regardless of your wishes.

WANGEL   I'm sorry?

ELLIDA   Make him leave.
Please, you have to make him leave.

WANGEL   (*To* ELLIDA.) Hilde said that a man had
              come to the house.
              Asking for you.

STRANGER   (*To* ELLIDA.) The ship will be ready for you.

WANGEL   She said his name was Alfred Johnson.

STRANGER   That's not my name any more.

WANGEL   What is it then?
              What is your name, stranger?
              Too cowardly to even tell me?

STRANGER   I meant what I said, Ellida.
              If you wish it, you'll come with me tomorrow.

WANGEL   What does he mean?

STRANGER   And if not...
              It will be the last time you see me.

              THE STRANGER *turns to go*.

ELLIDA   Wait.

              THE STRANGER *turns back*.

              The last time?

STRANGER   I'll come tomorrow at seven.

ELLIDA   But –

STRANGER   And you will have made your choice.

WANGEL   What choice?

              THE STRANGER *looks at* WANGEL.

              Looks at him properly for the first time.

              He gestures to his hand.

STRANGER   (*To* WANGEL.) You think that ring around
              your finger makes you safe.
              But it doesn't prove a thing.
              The sea will carry the promise we made to
              one another forever.

He turns to go.

WANGEL   Forever?
                That's nonsense!
                You read her letters.
                That promise is meaningless to her.
                She's forgotten it.

STRANGER   The sea is stronger than a band of gold around
                your finger.

WANGEL   But you were children!
                It meant nothing!

STRANGER   Nothing, you say?

WANGEL   It was juvenile folly!
                Island mumbo-jumbo!

STRANGER   (*To* ELLIDA.) Tomorrow.
                I'll return for you.

WANGEL   What are you going to do?
                Take her by force?

STRANGER   There will be no force here.

WANGEL   Oh really?
                You think I don't know?
                You think I don't know exactly the kind of
                man you are?

STRANGER   What use is force?
                This isn't about that.
                This is about choice.

                He looks at ELLIDA.

                Your choice, Ellida.
                Your choice alone.

ELLIDA   Mine?

WANGEL   I saw that captain when you were finished
                with him.
                And I saw his wife and children too.

The way they wept with grief.
It's disgusting.
That you've roamed free for so long while
they've lived in agony.
It's amoral.

STRANGER   (*To* ELLIDA.) You have to come of your own
free will.
Do you hear me?
Or, if you choose to stay.
That must be your choice too.
Yours and no one else's.

THE STRANGER *looks at* WANGEL.

(*To* ELLIDA.) Tomorrow night.
Wait for me here.
Alone.

He climbs over the fence.

Goodbye, mermaid.

THE STRANGER *exits.*

ELLIDA *and* WANGEL *are alone.*

WANGEL   That's him?
The man you loved.

ELLIDA   Yes.

She looks at where THE STRANGER *was.*

WANGEL   If you'd seen what I'd seen.
That captain, what was left of him.
Ellida, you'd realise.
You'd realise what he is.

ELLIDA   Did you hear what he said?
My own free will.

WANGEL   He's dangerous.
Surely you can see that.

ELLIDA   Yes.

WANGEL	And you're afraid of him.
ELLIDA	Yes.
WANGEL	Well then. It's decided. We'll go to the police. Tell them where to find him. He'll be shoved behind bars, where he belongs –
ELLIDA	No.
WANGEL	No?
ELLIDA	Lock him up? It would kill him.
WANGEL	But if we don't...
ELLIDA	He has to be free. He belongs out there. Don't you understand?

LYNGSTRAND *and* HILDE *enters*.

LYNGSTRAND	There you are! You won't believe this!
WANGEL	Not now, Lyngstrand –
LYNGSTRAND	The man I was telling you about, Ellida! The one who inspired my sculpture!
WANGEL	Lyngstrand –
LYNGSTRAND	I saw him! Walking along the road, bold as anything! I could have sworn he was dead!
HILDE	He came to the house. I opened the door to him. He smelt of the sea.
WANGEL	You mustn't answer the door to him again. Do you hear me?

HILDE	I'll let him in through my bedroom window.
LYNGSTRAND	He's come for his wife. He's come to seek revenge on her. For her faithlessness!
WANGEL	What are you talking about?
HILDE	It's Lyngstrand's sculpture.
WANGEL	What?
HILDE	The looming man with the hands like crab's claws –
LYNGSTRAND	Oh this is wonderful! This has inspired me! I need to get to my studio immediately! Imagine if I could get him to pose for me… Hey! Wait! Alfred Johnson!

He exits.

HILDE *follows him.*

WANGEL *and* ELLIDA *are alone.*

ELLIDA	I know it for sure now.
WANGEL	Know what?
ELLIDA	He'll never let me go.

She gazes in the direction of the sea.

It's almost as if I can smell it again…
The sea.

She takes a step towards it.

WANGEL *follows her.*

Touches her shoulder.

She turns and looks at him.

Can you save me?

WANGEL   From what?

ELLIDA   Myself.

              She turns and stares towards the sea again.

ACT FOUR

A conservatory at the back of the house.

BOLETTE *is drawing something in her sketchbook.*

LYNGSTRAND *is peering at it over her shoulder.*

LYNGSTRAND Not bad.

> *She tries to cover what she is drawing with her hand.*

BOLETTE Don't look.

LYNGSTRAND No, honestly.
It's really not bad.

BOLETTE I'm just doodling.

LYNGSTRAND I think you could be bolder with it, though.
Make it a bit more abstract.

BOLETTE I'm not trying to be abstract.
It's just a sketch.

LYNGSTRAND I could lend you some interesting books.
I mean, if you're really serious about it.
Are you?

BOLETTE I don't know.
I like doing it.

LYNGSTRAND Then it's just a hobby.

BOLETTE So if I enjoy it then it isn't real?
It doesn't count?

LYNGSTRAND Enjoying it probably means you're not
pushing yourself enough.
You have to really suffer for good art.

BOLETTE   Do you suffer?

LYNGSTRAND   God yes.
                 It's torture.

BOLETTE   You seem to be having a nice enough time.

LYNGSTRAND   Oh but I am suffering.
                 You should see me when I'm in my studio.

BOLETTE   You mean Mrs Jensen's.

LYNGSTRAND   Yes.
                 Mrs Jensen's...
                 Come and visit if you like.
                 I mean, if you want.
                 Would you like to?

                 He looks at her.

                 A moment between them.

BOLETTE   Maybe.

LYNGSTRAND   I think what you need is someone to admire.
                 To inspire you.
                 Then you'd improve no end.

                 BOLETTE *scrumples up her piece of paper.*

                 You know, someone to look up to.
                 And then his talents and skills might be sort
                 of...
                 Passed on to you.
                 Through osmosis.

BOLETTE   I don't know about that.

LYNGSTRAND   You see it a lot actually.

BOLETTE   What?

LYNGSTRAND   The wives of great men.
                 Being a kind of mirror image of their
                 husbands.
                 Their exposure to his talents and skills means
                 they're able to develop their own.

	Which is as good an argument for marriage as I've ever heard. Do you want to?
BOLETTE	Do I want to what?
LYNGSTRAND	Get married.
BOLETTE	I haven't really thought about it that much.
LYNGSTRAND	What, really?! Girls I know are always rabbiting on about marriage. I was with this one girl for a bit who –
BOLETTE	So you're saying these wives miraculously transform into their husbands?
LYNGSTRAND	Well. Only in really exceptional marriages.
BOLETTE	And what about the other way around?
LYNGSTRAND	What do you mean?
BOLETTE	Could a husband be transformed into his wife? Pass on her talents and skills to him? Through osmosis?
LYNGSTRAND	Oh. Um...?
BOLETTE	Or does it only work in one direction?
LYNGSTRAND	Well, I suppose it does tend to be men who are more...
BOLETTE	What?
LYNGSTRAND	Ambitious. Cos, you know. Women are better at bucking people up. Men need a lot of support and encouragement. Women are good at that.
BOLETTE	So they don't have any ambitions of their own?

LYNGSTRAND   I mean, they might have some.
              But usually it's about getting married and
              having babies and stuff.
              Making a really lovely home.
              Creating an environment where the man can
              really flourish.

BOLETTE   Do you have any idea how you sound?

LYNGSTRAND   What?

BOLETTE   And why do people have to be transformed
              into each other anyway?
              Can't people just stay individuals?
              Why would I want to be swallowed up whole
              by another person?
              That just sounds like cannibalism.

              Pause.

LYNGSTRAND   Sorry.

BOLETTE   It's all right.

LYNGSTRAND   You know, my...
              My mother was brilliant...
              Much more brilliant than my father ever was.
              I hated it when she died.

              He looks at her.

              We have that in common I suppose.

BOLETTE   Yes.
              I suppose we do.

              Pause.

LYNGSTRAND   Bolette?

BOLETTE   What?

LYNGSTRAND   When I'm gone...

BOLETTE   But you're much better!
              You're fine, in fact!
              Look at you!

LYNGSTRAND Oh I know that.
I'm talking about my trip to New York in
a few weeks.

BOLETTE Oh.
That.

LYNGSTRAND I expect it's possible I might be a bit –
Well.
Lonely out there.

BOLETTE But...
You'll be with people constantly.
All those people from the gallery and –

LYNGSTRAND What if...
What if they don't like my work?

BOLETTE They... Of course they will.

Pause.

LYNGSTRAND Do you like my work?

BOLETTE Yes.

LYNGSTRAND Do you?

Pause.

BOLETTE I don't know what to make of it.
If you want to know the truth.

LYNGSTRAND You see, this is why I like you.

BOLETTE Do you?

LYNGSTRAND Because you're honest.

Pause.

Will you promise to think of me?
When I'm away.

BOLETTE Think of you?

LYNGSTRAND It would cheer me up no end.
I think my sculpture would benefit hugely

	from knowing you were thinking about me. So will you?
BOLETTE	And that's all? Just… Think?
LYNGSTRAND	It would mean a lot.

Pause.

| BOLETTE | Yes all right.
I'll think about you.
Hans… |

He breaks into a smile.

After a moment she does as well.

Then she frowns and turns away.

But what's the point?

LYNGSTRAND	What do you mean?
BOLETTE	It will all come to nothing. Won't it?
LYNGSTRAND	No it won't. I'll write you letters. I'll tell you exactly how the sculpture is coming along. I'll enclose drawings –
BOLETTE	So this is all just about a sculpture, is it?
LYNGSTRAND	Well –
BOLETTE	Is it?

ARNHOLM *can be seen through the window
in the garden.*

BOLETTE *looks over at him.*

| LYNGSTRAND | Bolette – |
| BOLETTE | Shh.
Arnholm's coming. |

LYNGSTRAND   Him again.
             How much longer is he staying for?

BOLETTE   I don't know.
             As long as he likes.
             It's nice for Dad to have someone to talk to.

LYNGSTRAND   He seems to talk to you a fair bit as well.

BOLETTE   He takes an interest in my education.

LYNGSTRAND   Doesn't he have a family or anything?

BOLETTE   He's not married.
             If that's what you're getting at.

LYNGSTRAND   I'm not that surprised.
             Although I've heard he's rich.

BOLETTE   I suppose it's hard for him to meet someone.
             Considering he's taught most of the girls he
             knows at one point or another.

LYNGSTRAND   What about someone his own age?

BOLETTE   He's not that old.

LYNGSTRAND   He's a lot older than you.

             ARNHOLM *enters*.

ARNHOLM   (*To* BOLETTE.) Just the person I wanted
             to see!

             He notices LYNGSTRAND.

             Ah.
             Hello.

LYNGSTRAND   Hello.

ARNHOLM   Another visit!

LYNGSTRAND   Oh yes.

ARNHOLM   You certainly seem very at home here.

LYNGSTRAND   Indeed.
             So do you.

BOLETTE	Lyngstrand was giving me some tips. On abstract expressionism.
ARNHOLM	You've been drawing?
BOLETTE	Not really. Nothing worth revealing at any rate. Did you manage to speak to Dad?
ARNHOLM	Oh, Bolette. Sorry. I haven't had the chance... Yet.
BOLETTE	Right.
ARNHOLM	I did try. But he... I think he's a bit distracted at the moment.
BOLETTE	Makes a change.
ARNHOLM	I'll keep trying.
BOLETTE	No don't bother.
ARNHOLM	Of course I will. *Pause.* Has Ellida gone for her swim?
BOLETTE	No. She's just in her room.
ARNHOLM	Really? That's not like her.
BOLETTE	She's been up there for hours. She's locked herself in. WANGEL *enters.*
WANGEL	Arnholm. Just the man I was after.
BOLETTE	(*To* LYNGSTRAND.) Let's go and see what Hilde's up to.

LYNGSTRAND Do we have to?

BOLETTE Come on.

LYNGSTRAND *casts a combative look at* ARNHOLM.

He exits with BOLETTE.

ARNHOLM *and* WANGEL *are left alone.*

ARNHOLM What do you make of that boy?

WANGEL Hans?
There's no harm in him.

ARNHOLM He seems to be hanging around an awful lot.

WANGEL I feel rather sorry for him.
He's so obviously lonely.
And very unwell, of course.

ARNHOLM Do you mind him spending so much time with the girls?

WANGEL It's only natural, I suppose.
Why?
Do you think I should be keeping more of an eye on him?

ARNHOLM Perhaps it's more important to speak to the girls about that.

WANGEL Oh I don't know what I'd say...

ARNHOLM Bolette is really bright, you know.
I think she could make it to university.
Even somewhere in England, if you could spare her...?

Pause.

WANGEL You and Ellida have been spending time together.

ARNHOLM Yes.
Yes, a little.

WANGEL	What do you think? Am I missing something?
ARNHOLM	Missing what?
WANGEL	Am I just not looking hard enough? Is the answer staring me in the face?
ARNHOLM	I'm – Not sure.
WANGEL	I'm a doctor, aren't I? A good one, by all accounts.
ARNHOLM	Yes...
WANGEL	Surely I should be able to find a cure.
ARNHOLM	Perhaps it's not the kind of thing you cure...
WANGEL	Listen to me. I sound like a belligerent old tyrant, don't I? Trying to diagnose my own wife.
ARNHOLM	It's understandable...
WANGEL	Her mother, you know...
ARNHOLM	I know.
WANGEL	I can't help but wonder if... Worry...
ARNHOLM	Yes. I'd be the same.
WANGEL	You would?
ARNHOLM	You're trying to protect her.
WANGEL	But that seems to be the last thing she wants...

Pause.

Perhaps I just need to accept this in her.
Let whatever it is run its course.
Trust that the currents will turn and...
She'll be the same Ellida as before.

ARNHOLM   Perhaps she can't be.

WANGEL   You think she's gone for good?

ARNHOLM   Are you the same?
           The same man she met seven years ago?

WANGEL   I thought I was...
          Then again...
          I might do things differently now.

ARNHOLM   How so?

WANGEL   I was too quick to make her leave her home.
          Leave the sea...
          I should never have uprooted her.
          Forced her into a new habitat.
          I swept her back here without stopping to ask
          if she actually wanted to come.

ARNHOLM   But she did come.

WANGEL   Perhaps I didn't give her a choice.

ARNHOLM   Of course she had a choice.

WANGEL   She'd just lost her father.
          I should have waited.
          I should have given her time...
          But I was blinded to all of that out of sheer...
          Romantic recklessness.

ARNHOLM   Isn't that what romance does?
           Makes us reckless?

WANGEL   I've damaged something.
          I know I have.

ARNHOLM   You have to stop blaming yourself.

WANGEL   It's up to me to rectify it.
          That's why I asked you here.

ARNHOLM   Me?

WANGEL   I thought...
          If she saw you again...

Someone significant from her past...
Someone she perhaps still longed for in
some way...

ARNHOLM   What?

WANGEL   That I'd be giving back to her something that
I...
That I'd stolen.

ARNHOLM   You asked me here because of –
Because of Ellida?

WANGEL   In giving you back to her I could...
Atone.
Make amends.

ARNHOLM   It was Ellida who you thought was...
Longing for me?

WANGEL   Yes.
Who else would it have been?

ARNHOLM   No.
No one, of course.

WANGEL   But it seems I was wrong.
It wasn't you at all.

ARNHOLM   No.

Pause.

I'm sorry.
Not to have been more help...
On that front.

WANGEL   Ah well.
It was only an idea...

ARNHOLM   You would do that?
Honestly?
Sacrifice yourself in that way?

WANGEL   I just want her to be happy.

Pause.

ARNHOLM   This will pass.

WANGEL   Will it?

ARNHOLM   Of course.

WANGEL   I don't know.
          This man...
          I can't explain it...
          There's something almost...

ARNHOLM   Almost what?

WANGEL   Never mind.
          Forget I said anything.

ARNHOLM   He's just a man, Wangel.
          Less of a man than you are.

WANGEL   Not to her.

ARNHOLM   But – !
          All this stuff about the child's eyes!

WANGEL   She says it all began three years ago.
          Exactly the time that this sailor discovered
          she was now married to me.

ARNHOLM   Yes but – !

WANGEL   She's convinced, convinced...
          That the two things are connected.

ARNHOLM   But her unhappiness began rather earlier than
          that...?
          Didn't it?

WANGEL   You're right.
          There were signs and hints and, and...
          You're absolutely right.

ARNHOLM   There you are, you see – !

WANGEL   But –
          There was something.
          Something else.

ARNHOLM   What?

WANGEL   It was summer.
             July.
             When she was only a few months pregnant...

ARNHOLM   What?

             Pause.

WANGEL   Bolette found her.
             At the bottom of the stairs.

ARNHOLM   God.

WANGEL   She denied it.
             She said she slipped.

             Pause.

ARNHOLM   This is surmountable.
             You could move somewhere else.
             Move closer to the sea.
             Move back to where she grew up.

WANGEL   Do you think I haven't suggested that?

ARNHOLM   And?

WANGEL   She won't.

ARNHOLM   So then she's – !
             She's deliberately refusing to be happy!

WANGEL   She says it won't do any good.

ARNHOLM   Why?
             Why is she so unwilling to at least *try* to help
             herself?!

WANGEL   And anyway.
             I'd hate to unsettle the girls.
             They're so attached to this place...
             It would be like losing their mother all over
             again.

ARNHOLM   But –
             Forgive me, but –

They're nearly adults.
Bolette certainly –

WANGEL   Please.
              Not that.
              Not that as well.
              Not today.

              Pause.

ARNHOLM   But you and Ellida can't go on like this.

WANGEL   I know.

ARNHOLM   So…?
              What are you going to do?
              You have to fight, Wangel!
              This selflessness is all well and good, but –

WANGEL   What do I do, Arnholm?
              Barricade the door?
              Tell her she needs to pull herself together?
              Buck up?

ARNHOLM   You just have to stand your ground.
              Be a man.

WANGEL   I detest that phrase.
              My father was always saying it…

              ELLIDA *enters.*

              They stand up when they see her.

              Your hair's dry.

ELLIDA   No, I didn't go today.

              Silence.

              ARNHOLM *looks at* WANGEL *and*
              ELLIDA.

              Clears his throat.

ARNHOLM   I think I'll go and see what the girls are up to!

ELLIDA	I don't know where they are. I never can keep track of them.

ARNHOLM exits.

ELLIDA and WANGEL look at one another.

It's eleven o'clock.

WANGEL	Yes.
ELLIDA	So in eight hours he'll be back.
WANGEL	If we're to believe him.
ELLIDA	I believe him.

Pause.

She points to his hand.

Why do you wear that ring?

WANGEL	Of course I wear it. It's my wedding ring. It's precious.
ELLIDA	Why do we do that to one another?
WANGEL	Do what?
ELLIDA	Enclose.

Pause.

WANGEL	But… Marriage is… It's what people do.
ELLIDA	Why?
WANGEL	Because it's… Serious. Ceremonial. Important. It makes you stronger.
ELLIDA	How does it make you stronger?

WANGEL	Because without it, then…
ELLIDA	Then?
WANGEL	Nothing's fixed. It could all slip away at any moment.
	They look at one another.
ELLIDA	From the moment I put this ring on my finger I felt…
WANGEL	What?
ELLIDA	As if you'd bought me.
WANGEL	Bought you?
ELLIDA	I sold myself to you.
WANGEL	No.
ELLIDA	I'm not blaming you. It was a transaction we made together.
WANGEL	A transaction.
ELLIDA	I became property. Chattel.
WANGEL	I have never. Never. In any way. Thought of you as my property.
ELLIDA	It's not just you. It's everyone. The island. The whole world.
WANGEL	So love plays no part in it? None at all?
ELLIDA	Love doesn't need this.
	She lifts up her hand.
	She starts to take off her ring.

WANGEL	What are you doing?
ELLIDA	Will you take yours off too?
WANGEL	No! No, I won't.
ELLIDA	Please, Wangel.
WANGEL	Of course I won't. I can't –
ELLIDA	If you let me go –
WANGEL	No.
ELLIDA	Then we can both be free.
WANGEL	I don't want to be free.
ELLIDA	I need to have my full freedom. Do you understand?

She starts to pull the ring off.

He seizes her hand.

WANGEL	Please. Not yet. Please don't do that yet.
ELLIDA	A freely given promise is just as valid as this. More so.
WANGEL	That strange ceremony where you threw your rings into the sea? That can't compete with this!
ELLIDA	That was real. That was pure.
WANGEL	That wasn't a marriage.
ELLIDA	We made a vow to one another.
WANGEL	You made a vow to me. A real one.
ELLIDA	So let me go back on it.

WANGEL   So you're asking for a divorce?
          Is that it?

ELLIDA   I don't care what we call it.

WANGEL   I'm pretty sure that's what it's called.

ELLIDA   All I ask is that I'm free to choose.
          I can't let my lack of freedom make the
          choice for me.
          I can't hide behind the fact of being another
          man's wife.

WANGEL   What choice?

ELLIDA   To either stay here with you.
          Or...

WANGEL   Or go with him?

          Pause.

          I can't let you make that choice.
          I can't.

ELLIDA   Then you'll make this harder than it needs
          to be.

WANGEL   You know nothing about this man.
          Nothing!
          He's a pirate, Ellida!
          What kind of husband –
          What kind of *man* would I be –
          If I let you run into the arms of someone who
          is almost certain to be the end of you?

ELLIDA   Maybe he will be the end of me.
          How can I know?
          How can I know unless you let me choose?

WANGEL   How can you even contemplate choosing
          someone –
          Something –
          That you readily admit might be the end
          of you?

ELLIDA   Haven't you ever longed for the thing that
              frightens you the most?
              Isn't that why we long for it?
              The unknown.
              The glorious horror…

              He looks at her.

WANGEL   I long for you.
              And more and more I realise that you are…
              Completely unknown to me.

              They look at one another.

              Please let me help you.
              Let me give you the strength and support you
              need to fight this.

ELLIDA   I don't want to fight it.

WANGEL   It's my duty, as your husband, to protect you.

ELLIDA   Am I really so fragile?

WANGEL   Yes!

ELLIDA   Yes?

WANGEL   Let me speak to you as your doctor.

ELLIDA   My doctor.

WANGEL   You are unwell.
              Very unwell.
              You have been for some time.
              You are not in a fit state to make decisions for
              yourself.

              Silence.

              Slowly she lets go of his hand.

ELLIDA   You can lock the doors if you want.
              You can weld this ring onto my flesh.
              If that would make you happy.
              But you know, deep down, it would make no
              difference to what I long for.

WANGEL	To throw yourself into the sea? Regardless of where it takes you?
ELLIDA	I think that's where I belong.
WANGEL	You belong here! With me!
ELLIDA	Or perhaps I belong with him.
HILDE	(*Off.*) Dad!

WANGEL *turns away from* ELLIDA.

WANGEL	And what about the girls? Where do they fit into all of this?
ELLIDA	The girls...
WANGEL	You haven't considered them, have you? Perhaps you never have.
ELLIDA	That isn't fair.
WANGEL	They were so happy, when I said I was bringing you home with me. A new mother! But I suppose you don't care about them. In the same way you don't care about me. You only care about yourself.

BOLETTE, HILDE *and* ARNHOLM *enter,*
 in swimsuits.

HILDE	We're going to the lagoon!
ARNHOLM	They've persuaded me to go swimming!
HILDE	We're going to take the inflatables and just lie sprawled on the water all day. Lyngstrand won't come. He's so boring.
BOLETTE	He wasn't feeling well.
HILDE	I think his whole illness is a lie to get people to feel sorry for him.

WANGEL	Girls.
ARNHOLM	Will you two join us for the day?
	He looks warily at WANGEL *and* ELLIDA.
WANGEL	Girls, come here.
	HILDE *and* BOLETTE *look at each other.*
	Slowly they go to WANGEL.
	He takes both of their hands.
	Your stepmother and I have… We've been making some plans and…
	He looks at ELLIDA.
HILDE	What? Why are you looking at her like that?
WANGEL	It's possible that… She'll be leaving us for a while.
HILDE	No!
WANGEL	It's possible that… That both of us will go.
BOLETTE	Both of you?
WANGEL	(*Looking at* ELLIDA.) Yes. Ellida wants to go home. To the sea. And I will go with her.
ELLIDA	Wangel. Please.
HILDE	(*To* ELLIDA.) Why are you still here? Why not just leave now if that's what you want to do? Go on.
	HILDE *runs away.*
	BOLETTE *turns to* WANGEL.

BOLETTE	You'd choose her over us…?
ARNHOLM	Bolette…
ELLIDA	That's not what your father is doing. I promise –
BOLETTE	(*To* ELLIDA.) Don't you realise what Hilde has wanted more than anything else? From the second you set foot in this house?
ELLIDA	What?
BOLETTE	For you to see her and love her.
ELLIDA	I – I do love her…
BOLETTE	It's too late for that now.
WANGEL	(*To* ARNHOLM.) Forget the lagoon. Take a trip to the Marina with me instead. In fact, let's all go! Bolette, come on.
BOLETTE	No thank you.
WANGEL	Yes yes, we should all go. We'll raise a toast. To The Lady from the Sea. Let's go and drink and dance till the sun comes up! What are you all waiting for? Why are you all looking at me like that? Let's go!

ACT FIVE

The garden.

Evening.

ELLIDA *is staring out towards the lakes.*

WANGEL *enters.*

She doesn't turn around.

He goes over to her, thinks about placing his hand on her shoulder.

Decides against it.

He goes and sits slightly apart from her.

ELLIDA *turns and sees him.*

They look at each other.

She turns back to the water.

ELLIDA	Not long now.
WANGEL	There's still time.
	He watches her.
	Will you come and sit by me? Just for a moment?
	She continues to stare out.
	BALLESTRED *enters, carrying a steel pan.*
BALLESTRED	Good evening, Mr and Mrs Wangel! Another day in paradise drawing to a close!
WANGEL	You're always so industrious, Ballestred. You put the rest of us to shame.

BALLESTRED   Oh I'm an amateur.
              Not a professional like you, Dr Wangel.
              But I'm an amateur with passion!

WANGEL   I hear you're going to be performing later on
              tonight.

BALLESTRED   You've heard correctly!
              The Hollywood Actor has requested a special
              performance to mark the start of Carnival.
              It seems words of my talent have spread even
              to his gilded ears!

WANGEL   I don't doubt it.

BALLESTRED   You must come!
              He would be delighted to welcome you on
              board, I'm sure of it!
              Especially if I informed him that you were
              very special friends of mine.

ELLIDA   So his yacht has arrived?

BALLESTRED   I believe they took the day to visit the
              neighbouring islands.
              And so, if my calculations are correct...
              The boat will be arriving in the harbour any
              moment now!

              They look in the direction of the harbour.

              The boat is there.

              Would you look at that?
              I've got quite the gift, wouldn't you agree?

ELLIDA   It's always like that.
              One minute it's empty and the next...

BALLESTRED   It will be empty again soon enough,
              Mrs Wangel.
              You'll have the lagoon back to yourself.

WANGEL   I hear The Actor won't be returning next year.

BALLESTRED   Yes, it appears he's turned that piercing blue
              gaze elsewhere now.
              Ah well.
              Endings are inevitable.
              But that doesn't make them any easier to take.
              I confess to growing a little melancholy at this
              time of year.

ELLIDA   The end of the season is always strange.

BALLESTRED   Yes indeed.
              Knowing the winds are coming.
              Knowing the harbour will soon be empty.
              Ah well.
              There's always next year.
              And the year after that…!
              Good Lord, is that the time?!
              I have a band to warm up!
              Adieu, adieu!

              BALLESTRED exits.

ELLIDA   He'll be here soon then.
              Any moment.

              She looks at her ring.

              WANGEL *sees her doing it.*

              He takes her hand.

              You've never asked me to do a single thing in
              this house.
              Do you know that?
              You've never even given me a key.

              Pause.

WANGEL   I suppose I got used to it being just the three
              of us…
              We muddled along and…
              We made it through.
              Somehow.

ELLIDA	You didn't think I could help you?
WANGEL	You'd been through so much yourself. I didn't want to burden you.
ELLIDA	Or you didn't think I was capable.
WANGEL	No, it was never that.
ELLIDA	What then?
WANGEL	I didn't think it appealed to you. Domesticity.
ELLIDA	I'm not talking about domesticity. I'm talking about responsibility.
WANGEL	Whose?
ELLIDA	Mine! Bolette has more responsibility than me. Perhaps that's why I've always thought of myself as just another one of the children. But the truth is I'm much, much older than the girls, Wangel.
WANGEL	I know that.
ELLIDA	So I'm going to ask you one more time. To let me make this choice as a free woman.
WANGEL	I can't do it.
ELLIDA	But you understand that... That if you don't give me what I ask for. Then the choice I make will be a false one?
WANGEL	It's too much. Too much to ask of me, Ellida. I can't.
ELLIDA	(*Pointing to her ring*.) Why do you want to strangle me with this? Contain me. Contain the things I long for.

WANGEL   I know I can't contain them…

ELLIDA   Then why do you hold onto me so tightly?
                It's as if you know that, once you let go…
                There's nothing here to ground me.
                I'll just float away.
                Because I'm completely rootless here, Wangel.

WANGEL   But you've been happy here before!
                You could be again.
                I'll build you another arbour.
                I'll give you a thousand keys.
                I'll do whatever you want – !

ELLIDA   I want to live all the life it is possible to live.
                I just want to be allowed to live it.
                To choose it!

                Pause.

WANGEL   Come on.
                Let's walk a little longer.

ELLIDA   There isn't time.

WANGEL   There is.
                Let's see if we can spot any hummingbirds
                over by the pond.

ELLIDA   You're still so kind to me.

                She turns and stares towards the lakes.

                Then turns back to him.

                She takes his hand.

                ARNHOLM *and* BOLETTE *enter.*

ARNHOLM   There you are – !

BOLETTE   Shh.
                Let them go.

                They watch as ELLIDA *and* WANGEL *exit.*

ARNHOLM   How do you feel about it?
                Ellida going away for a while…?

BOLETTE   Please.
             You and I both know that if she goes, she'll
             be gone for good.

ARNHOLM   You sound envious.

BOLETTE   Of course I'm envious.
             To leave, to be free, to do whatever she
             chooses.

ARNHOLM   You're free.
             To do whatever you choose.

             Pause.

BOLETTE   So did you speak to Dad?

ARNHOLM   Well..

BOLETTE   Did you?

ARNHOLM   I…
             I tried.

             Pause.

BOLETTE   So.
             Then you understand.

ARNHOLM   You mustn't take it personally.
             He's.
             He's preoccupied at the moment.

BOLETTE   He always is.

ARNHOLM   There's a lot in flux for him.
             It's hard for him to imagine he might lose you
             as well.

BOLETTE   And you stand there and tell me I'm free to do
             as I choose?

             Pause.

ARNHOLM   What if I was to help you?

BOLETTE   How do you mean?

ARNHOLM   Exactly what I say.

BOLETTE   Help me?
           How?

ARNHOLM   Well.
           What is it you need?

           Pause.

           Is it money?

BOLETTE   No...

ARNHOLM   Bolette...

BOLETTE   Dad has fewer and fewer patients these days.
           He spends all his time at the surgery but...
           I think he only does that to get away from us.

ARNHOLM   Very well.
           Money, I can offer.

BOLETTE   Arnholm.
           You can't –

ARNHOLM   Contacts too.
           I've got friends at all sorts of universities in
           England.

BOLETTE   England?

ARNHOLM   Wouldn't you like to go to Oxford?
           Take a punt along the river?
           In a jaunty boater?

BOLETTE   They don't do that really, do they?

ARNHOLM   Oh they do.
           All the time.
           It's quite insufferable.

           She looks at him, not sure whether to smile.

           Would you like me to speak to some people.
           See what I can do?
           You could be there for the start of the new term.

BOLETTE	It's – It's too late in the year…
ARNHOLM	Well, I could pull some strings. If it's what you really want to do…?
BOLETTE	Of course it is. It's all I want. But –
ARNHOLM	Well then. Let yourself accept what I'm offering.
BOLETTE	But it doesn't change anything. Don't you see? There's still Dad…

Pause.

ARNHOLM	He has to let you go eventually.
BOLETTE	It's not that simple.
ARNHOLM	If you were to turn round to him and say – Dad. I'm leaving. I'm going to go and get a degree and meet new people and push at the very boundaries of my mind. This very brilliant mind I've been lucky enough to inherit from you.
BOLETTE	But –
ARNHOLM	Then I promise he will be nothing but delighted for you. The last thing he wants is to keep you here against your will.
BOLETTE	I don't know…
ARNHOLM	For goodness' sake, Bolette! Allow yourself to be happy!

She takes a deep breath.

BOLETTE   It would be…
           Good.
           To get away.

ARNHOLM   There you are.
           See!

BOLETTE   To be stimulated and challenged and…
           To be able to ask questions and have someone
           answer me for a change!
           Not just pat me on the head and tell me to
           relax and enjoy the sun.

ARNHOLM   Yes!

BOLETTE   Imagine!
           Just to get on a boat and – !
           Set sail!
           For England!

ARNHOLM   That's the spirit!

BOLETTE   It would be so…
           So painfully wonderful.
           But…

           Pause.

           It would break his heart.

           ARNHOLM *turns away.*

ARNHOLM   Is it just your dad you're talking about?
           No one else?

BOLETTE   No.

ARNHOLM   Are you sure?

BOLETTE   Very –
           Very sure.

           Pause.

           What is it?

ARNHOLM   Very well.
           I need to just say this because…

Because if I don't then I'll regret it for ever,
possibly, and, you only get one life.
Don't you?
And.
Well.
I'm not getting any younger.
And if there's anything this trip has taught me
it's that you have to seize life with both
hands, when it's presented to you.
And I may be going right out on a limb here
but...
But if I don't say it then...
Then...

BOLETTE   Say what?

Pause.

ARNHOLM   I think it's possible that I've fallen in love
with you, Bolette.
And that I'd like, really quite badly...
To marry you.

Pause.

BOLETTE   Oh.

They both wait.

ARNHOLM   I can see I've shocked you.

BOLETTE   No, I...
Sorry.
I mean.
You're my tutor.

ARNHOLM   Was your tutor.

BOLETTE   But...

ARNHOLM   Fine, yes.
That's all we were to one another.
Once.

BOLETTE   I mean, I was thirteen...

ARNHOLM   How would you feel if I told you that the
           whole…
           Reason I travelled out here was because…
           Because of you?

BOLETTE   *Is* that what you're telling me…?

ARNHOLM   Your father wrote me a letter last spring.
           He told me there was a young woman here
           who he believed to be…
           Yearning.
           For me.

BOLETTE   But –
           Why on earth would he – ?
           I never said anything to – !

ARNHOLM   No, no, you're right, I got it completely wrong.
           Barking up the wrong tree entirely, as it
           happens.
           But!
           Ever since I got that letter I found that I was
           just –
           Entirely –
           Consumed by you.

BOLETTE   Arnholm, I…

ARNHOLM   Consumed with imagining the kind of woman
           you might have become.
           It awoke something in me.
           Something that I hadn't felt since…
           A very long time before.
           And now that I'm here, and I've spent time
           with you, and I've seen at first hand just how
           extraordinary and kind and clever and –
           And beautiful you are.
           No, you are, don't protest.
           I don't know if I'll ever be able to…
           To close myself off to it.

           They look at each other.

Could you ever...
Bolette?
Do you think that you could ever...
Learn to see me in that light?
Is it possible?

Silence.

BOLETTE   I –

Pause.

I'm very fond of you.

ARNHOLM   Ah.

BOLETTE   But...

Pause.

ARNHOLM   Of course.
I completely understand.

BOLETTE   It's just –
Perhaps if you hadn't been my tutor then...

ARNHOLM   Well.
The important thing is that you get to realise
your dream.
I'll get in touch with those friends of mine, as
I mentioned.

BOLETTE   You don't have to do that for me.

ARNHOLM   No I want to.
It would be my pleasure.

BOLETTE   I can't accept a gesture like that if...

ARNHOLM   If what?

BOLETTE   If I doubt the motivation.

Pause.

ARNHOLM   Bolette.
Please don't misinterpret me.

My motivation here is purely that you are able
to do the things you crave.
The things you deserve.
I've –
I've told you how I feel and…
And you don't feel the same.
Very well.
That's that.

BOLETTE   I…

ARNHOLM   What I can't bear is for you to miss out.
On life!
You deserve all the life you can possibly get
your hands on, Bolette!
Don't let the blatherings of a sentimental
old fool prevent you from plunging into it
head first.

Pause.

BOLETTE   You've really revealed something to me in the
last few days.
About myself.
Uncomfortable things.

ARNHOLM   Oh?

BOLETTE   That I'm my own worst enemy.
That I make excuses.
That I'm terrified –
Terrified…
Of failure.

ARNHOLM   I hope I haven't been too heavy-handed.

BOLETTE   No.
I needed to be told.
Thank you.

Pause.

Perhaps, in time, I…
I might be able to…

I could grow to…
Think of you.
In that light.

ARNHOLM   Really?

BOLETTE   Perhaps.
Yes.

ARNHOLM   I would hate to think that you…
Were entering into anything that you
weren't…
Completely comfortable with –

BOLETTE   I need time.

ARNHOLM   Yes.
Yes of course.

BOLETTE   But…
But if you were prepared to wait then
perhaps…

ARNHOLM   Yes.
I'll wait as long as you…
However long you need, Bolette.

BOLETTE   You're right.
I've side-stepped life for too long and now
I just have to –
Close my eyes and just –

ARNHOLM   Jump.

They smile at each other.

BOLETTE   So many of the boys I know…
They seem to just.
They don't want us to be free to be who we
really are.
They just want us to be a duller, weaker
versions of themselves.
But you're not like that.
You want me to go out into the world and –
Live life.

ARNHOLM   Yes.

BOLETTE   I couldn't be with someone who wants to put
me on a plinth.
Imprison me in a painting.
It's flattering at first, to be seen like that,
but...
I'd go mad, after a while.

LYNGSTRAND   (*Off.*) Why are we back here, Hilde?

HILDE   (*Off.*) I've told you!
I need to put on a different dress!
I'm sweating all over!

ARNHOLM   Our resident hypochondriac returns.

BOLETTE   He's not a hypochondriac.
It's real.

ARNHOLM   He seems healthy enough to me.

BOLETTE   No.
He probably won't make it out of his
twenties.
And I think that's probably for the best.

ARNHOLM   What do you mean?

BOLETTE   Because he dreams of glittering success.
But deep down he knows that he's a terrible
artist.
That his art will die when he does.
Oh it's too depressing.
Let's go before they get here.

ARNHOLM   I thought you'd never ask.

BOLETTE   Arnholm?

ARNHOLM   Yes?

BOLETTE   Don't say anything to anyone.
About...
Will you?

ARNHOLM	I promise.

ARNHOLM and BOLETTE *exit.*

LYNGSTRAND and HILDE *enter.*

LYNGSTRAND	Bolette – !
HILDE	Don't.
LYNGSTRAND	We should ask her to join us –
HILDE	No. Let them go.

She gazes after BOLETTE *and* ARNHOLM.

It's alarming.
The way he's always hanging around her
like that.
I'm surprised Dad hasn't said anything.

LYNGSTRAND	What's he got to say? There's nothing going on between them.
HILDE	You're so naive.
LYNGSTRAND	What?
HILDE	He's seducing her. It's desperately inappropriate. He's seventeen years older than she is.
LYNGSTRAND	I don't believe he's actually seducing –
HILDE	He is.
LYNGSTRAND	And anyway. Even if he thinks that's what he's doing. He wouldn't succeed.
HILDE	He might.
LYNGSTRAND	I very much doubt it.
HILDE	A girl can get past a receding hairline, you know. There are other things, below the surface… That are more interesting to us…

LYNGSTRAND   But she can't get past feeling things for
              someone else.
              That I do know.

HILDE   She's feeling things for someone else?

LYNGSTRAND   She's as much as said that there's only one
              man she's interested in.

HILDE   You, I suppose?

LYNGSTRAND   Yes.

              They look at each other.

              *Hold the gaze for a little longer than is
              comfortable.*

              HILDE *is the first to break it.*

HILDE   So that's it then?
              You two will go off and get married.
              'To love and to cherish.'
              'In sickness and in health.'
              Happily ever after.
              The end.

LYNGSTRAND   I wouldn't say that.
              There's nothing formal about it.
              I hate all of that rubbish.
              It's so bourgeois.

HILDE   What then?

LYNGSTRAND   I asked her to think about me.
              When I'm in New York.

HILDE   Think about you?

LYNGSTRAND   Yes.

HILDE   What does that mean?

LYNGSTRAND   To help me with my art.

HILDE   Bolette thinking about you is going to help
              you with your art?

LYNGSTRAND   Of course it is.
That's the whole point of a muse.

HILDE   Does she know that's what she is?

LYNGSTRAND   Of course.

HILDE   I wouldn't be so sure.

LYNGSTRAND   I can't really commit to anything long term
when my career is on the cusp of taking off!
Bolette knows that.
She understands.

HILDE   Bolette, Bolette, Bolette...

LYNGSTRAND   And anyway.
By the time I'm back, well, she'll be quite
a bit older by then and...
I don't know if the attraction will be as
strong.
Attraction is a very ephemeral thing.
You just can't guarantee if it will be there
or not.

He looks at HILDE.

HILDE   What?

LYNGSTRAND   You're quite clever, aren't you?

HILDE   Oh, clever.
Yes I know I'm clever.

LYNGSTRAND   I meant it as a compliment.

HILDE   Being clever's easy.
It's being desirable that's hard.

LYNGSTRAND   Everyone has a different idea of what
desirable is.

HILDE   There's only one way to be desirable if you're
a woman.

He looks at her.

So we learn to use tricks.
We learn the colours that suit us.
How to style our hair.
How to put red on our cheeks and black on
our eyes.

LYNGSTRAND This dress certainly suits you...
Very nicely...

HILDE I'm going to dress all in black from now on.

LYNGSTRAND Black is always very –
Elegant.

HILDE Frightening too.

LYNGSTRAND Frightening?

HILDE I'll have a long black veil.
It will go all the way down my back and trail
on the floor.

LYNGSTRAND I'd like to paint you in that.
I'd call it, 'The Grieving Widow'.

HILDE No.
'The Grieving Bride'.

She holds his gaze a little longer.

Turns away.

Look.

LYNGSTRAND What?

HILDE The Actor's yacht is back on the lagoon.
Come down there with me?
We can try and sneak our way onboard and
into the bar.
I've done it before.

LYNGSTRAND I don't know...

HILDE The music will start any moment.

Music starts.

See?

She takes his hand.

LYNGSTRAND   Yes.
Yes all right.

WANGEL and ELLIDA enter.

WANGEL   He isn't here.
He hasn't come.

ELLIDA   Wait.

She turns.

THE STRANGER *is there.*

STRANGER   So Ellida.
Here we are.

ELLIDA   Yes.

STRANGER   Are you coming with me?

WANGEL   You can see for yourself.
She has no bags packed.

THE STRANGER *notices* WANGEL *as if for the first time.*

STRANGER   Why is he here?

ELLIDA   This concerns him too.

STRANGER   I told you.
That you had to make this choice of your own free will.

A ship's bell rings.

There goes the first bell.
What will it be?
Yes.
Or no.

She takes a step towards him.

He holds out his hand.

She stops.

ELLIDA   Why?
            Why do you hold on to me still?
            After all this time?

STRANGER   You made me promise.

ELLIDA   But that was twenty years ago.

STRANGER   We belong to one another.

ELLIDA   You've made me wait.
            For twenty years...

STRANGER   I'm here now.

ELLIDA   You said you would come for me.

STRANGER   And I have.

ELLIDA   I was sixteen!

STRANGER   You haven't changed.

ELLIDA   I'm nearly forty.
            I'm nothing like the girl you knew then.
            Half my life is gone!

STRANGER   I have kept my promise.
            You broke yours.
            The ring on your finger tells me that.

ELLIDA   Do you know what it's like?
            To be sixteen years old and lose your mother?
            Then lose the first man who ever kissed you,
            touched you?
            The first man who ever really seemed to
            see you?
            The first man I ever truly saw.
            Oh God, I can smell the sea...

            She looks into his eyes.

            THE STRANGER *climbs over the fence.*

STRANGER   I've made my cabin ready for you, Ellida.
            If you come with me now, we can leave
            tonight.

She takes a step towards him.

ELLIDA   Be on the sea for ever.

STRANGER   Yes.

ELLIDA   Never set foot on land.
              Never again.

STRANGER   Never.
              If that's what you wish.

              He holds out his hand to her.

              She takes another step.

WANGEL   Wait, wait!

              They turn and look at him.

              (*To* THE STRANGER.) If you leave with my
              wife on that ship then –
              Then I will have no choice but to tell the
              authorities the truth.

STRANGER   And what is that?

WANGEL   You haven't got a chance.
              They lock people up for life for what you did.

STRANGER   I didn't do anything that wasn't justified.

WANGEL   Justified?!
              You're nothing but a butcher.
              You deserve to rot in prison.
              I can make that happen and I will.

              THE STRANGER *pulls a gun from his
              pocket.*

              He points it at WANGEL.

ELLIDA   Put the gun down…

              THE STRANGER *keeps the gun trained on*
              WANGEL.

              ELLIDA *steps in front of him.*

WANGEL   Ellida, no.

              ELLIDA *holds* THE STRANGER*'s gaze*.

              Slowly THE STRANGER *places the gun against his temple*.

STRANGER   This man has no power over me.
              I will live and die as a free man.

              The ship's bell sounds for a second time.

              So, Ellida?
              What do you say?
              Yes, or no?

              She stares at him, takes in the gun against his head.

ELLIDA   You're still just a boy.
              The same boy you were then.

STRANGER   We're running out of time.

ELLIDA   And that's what you want me to be.
              A girl.

STRANGER   Hurry.

ELLIDA   The same girl who ran into the sea with you.
              Lied to my father.
              Called him names and said I didn't love him any more.
              Because I only loved you.

              The bell sounds again.

              Neither of you...
              Neither of you can see me for what I really am.

WANGEL   Ellida...

ELLIDA   Look at me.
              Both of you.
              Look at me!

STRANGER   We don't have time for this.

ELLIDA   I can't be that girl any more.
            I don't want to be her.

WANGEL   My darling –

ELLIDA   I've grown old.

STRANGER   No.

ELLIDA   I'll grow older still.

STRANGER   Not out there.
            Not on the sea.

ELLIDA   But that's a fantasy.

STRANGER   No.

ELLIDA   I don't want a fantasy.
            I don't want to be one.

WANGEL   Ellida, listen –

ELLIDA   I want to be seen.
            That's all I ask for.
            Just.
            To be seen!

WANGEL   I see you.

            She turns to WANGEL.

            And so I'll let you go.

ELLIDA   You will?

WANGEL   You're free.

            Pause.

ELLIDA   If you let me go…

WANGEL   I do.

ELLIDA   But…
            You're taking a huge risk.

WANGEL   Yes.

ELLIDA	You would do that?
WANGEL	Yes.
ELLIDA	Why?
WANGEL	Because I love you.

The bell sounds again.

She looks back at THE STRANGER.

Takes a step away from him.

STRANGER	Ellida?
ELLIDA	That's your final bell. You can go now.
STRANGER	So... So it's over?
ELLIDA	I'm not afraid of you any more. I'm free.

He tries to take this in.

STRANGER	Where do I go?
ELLIDA	Back on the ship.
STRANGER	But... Who do I live for now?
ELLIDA	Someone real. Someone you actually see.
STRANGER	I see you.
ELLIDA	You did once.

THE STRANGER *stares at her.*

He climbs back over the fence.

STRANGER	You're a burning ship. You'll sink to the bottom and the fishes will eat you.

THE STRANGER *exits.*

ELLIDA *and* WANGEL *look at one another.*

ELLIDA

So.
Would you like to start again?
With me?

He goes to her.

WANGEL

I would.

ELLIDA

There can't be any pretence.

WANGEL

No.

ELLIDA

We can't try and be what we think the other person wants.

WANGEL

I promise.

ELLIDA

I'm flawed.
I'm fallible.

WANGEL

So am I.

ELLIDA

Can you forgive me?
For our son?

WANGEL

It wasn't your fault.

ELLIDA

It was.
Oh, it was.

WANGEL

No.

ELLIDA

But I couldn't...
He wouldn't...

WANGEL

You must promise me.
That you will stop blaming yourself.
Do you promise?

ELLIDA

It might be too late.
For another.

WANGEL

I know.

ELLIDA

Can you be happy?

WANGEL	Yes. Can you?

She looks at him.

ELLIDA	What you did for me just then…
WANGEL	I should have done it before. I'm sorry.
ELLIDA	Thank you.

ARNHOLM, BOLETTE, HILDE,
LYNGSTRAND *and* BALLESTRED *enter.*

ARNHOLM	Look. There goes that hideous yacht.
BALLESTRED	The season is truly over… Ah well.

They watch the ship sail away.

I hear that we're to lose you for a while,
Mrs Wangel.

ELLIDA	No. I'm staying here.
BOLETTE	What?
BALLESTRED	Well, this is very happy news!
HILDE	You're staying?
ELLIDA	If you'd like me to, Hilde?
HILDE	If you like. I don't mind…

She turns away, tries to hide her smile.

ELLIDA	(*To* ARNHOLM.) Do you remember, the other morning… I said that all our unhappiness began when we marooned ourselves on land?
BALLESTRED	Aha! Like the mermaid in my painting!

ARNHOLM   Of course.

ELLIDA   Perhaps it's time I gave the land a chance.

BALLESTRED   The mermaid in my painting dies.

WANGEL   Perhaps you might let her climb back onto the
               rocks, Ballestred.

BALLESTRED   It's certainly an idea.
               It would make for a far less gloomy painting!

ELLIDA   Yes.
               Give her responsibility for herself.
               Let her be free.

               WANGEL *and* ELLIDA *look at one another.*

WANGEL   Come on.
               Let's go to the harbour and watch the
               fireworks.
               I think they're about to begin.

               BALLESTRED, BOLETTE, HILDE *and*
               ARNHOLM *exit.*

               WANGEL *holds* ELLIDA *back.*

               Here.

               He takes off his ring.

               Holds out his hand, offering it to her.

               Let's find a new way to do this.
               Shall we?

               After a moment, ELLIDA *takes off her ring.*

               She is holding both the rings in her hand.

ELLIDA   Now what?

WANGEL   What do you think?

ELLIDA   We throw them into the sea.

               The End.

Other Titles in this Series

www.nickhernbooks.co.uk

 facebook.com/nickhernbooks

 twitter.com/nickhernbooks